Bonnie,
Aren't we glad we
moved on from Telus?
Way to be courageous
& live juicy!
Sherri

Crossroads Café:
Breaking free from the daily grind

Sherri Olsen & Val Lieske

Published by Sherri Olsen/Val Lieske
1-866-3-coach-9 www.sherriolsen.com
Coach@sherriolsen.com, 2002, Sherri Olsen/Val Lieske.
All rights reserved.

Cover by Deneen Tedeschini
Layout and Design by Jon Lyne

Printed and bound in Canada by BlitzPrint Canada

ISBN #0-9731865-0-x

Notes from the authors:

Sherri Olsen:

This book began as an idea to offer coaching in book form, at a low price to give people tools if they feel they are stuck in the daily grind. I had 40 pages written; but wanted it to read like a story, with characters we can all relate to. One was in the wrong job and scared to move, the other considering retirement and then gets downsized, one starting over after a divorce and needs a new career. My vision was a book that was easy to read, a great story, and filled with useful tools gained through conversation. I however, was not up for the challenge of being a fictional writer. And so the idea sat on my shelf for a period of time. Enter Val Lieske. Ex-banker, want to be theatre producer and writer, with all the reasons why her dream could not be a reality. So I asked her, why couldn't the successful writer or theatre producer be her? Someone will be. And then I asked the obvious, "what would it take for you to be a writer?" Duh, I'm sure she thought. "Um...well, I would have to write" was her response. "I have a project for you," I said, secretly hoping that she really could write. And write she can! Val created a wonderful story around characters that chat in a coffee shop and sort out their lives through discussions with their Life Coach. My dream then became a reality, as Vals did. Her story follows...

Val Lieske:

This book can change your life...it changed mine.
I wrote this book with Sherri the summer after I had been "right-sized" right out of my career of 13 years with a large financial institution. After sitting around for 3 months in my new flannel pajamas wondering "What just happened?" and "What now?" I finally decided I needed a change. A dramatic change. So I went in search of someone to help. Enter, Sherri, the Life Coach. She fell somewhere between a career counselor, psychiatrist and mother and she changed my life forever. She asked me the hard questions like, "What do you really, really want?" She made me solidify my goals and truly reinvent myself. Ultimately she changed my thinking, which changed my life.
After believing I was "only a banker" for most of my adult life, I decided to try a new character on - an artist. Even though I knew that wasn't a "real job". So, what happened in the year after I made that decision?
I went back to acting school, I started a theatre company - FIRE EXIT PRODUCTIONS, I began teaching at Rosebud School of the Arts, I am the regional promoter for a touring theatre company out of Toronto, I am Director of Theatre Arts at the largest church in Western Canada, I produced two shows for a college, I wrote and produced a one-woman show, "Gods Attention", oh yeah, and I wrote a book. Not too bad. Unemployment agrees with me!
I'm not that special, really. I just wanted a change, bad. If you want a change and are ready to let go of your good life in search of a great life...this is the book for you.

Val
Co-Author

CHAPTER ONE

I had been waiting almost fifteen minutes, and I could feel the irritation beginning to rise. Am I the only one who owns a watch? Relax, Sam, it's Saturday. I took a deep breath. I can't believe how uptight I've gotten. Letting the tension drain from my shoulders, I sipped my latté and flipped through the latest *People* magazine. The small coffee shop was unusually quiet for a sunny weekend morning. Glancing around the room, I was reminded again of how much I liked the décor. It was an old house that had been renovated, one of the few coffee shops located conveniently in a residential community. It had a character that most of the large coffee chains couldn't provide. Old hardwood floors, wrought-iron furniture, and large ceramic vases full of sunflowers gave the space a warm, comfortable feeling. I reached for a napkin and carefully folded it into a perfect square before bending down and slipping it under a leg of the wobbly table. It seemed to help. My fingers ran over the blue tiles in the tabletop, and I thought they looked like Scrabble tiles. I shifted uncomfortably on my chair with the too-straight back. The sound of the coffee grinder drowned out the opening of the wooden, screen door.

"I'm late, I'm late. I'm sorry!" Julie burst into the coffee shop with the usual aura of chaos following her. She had on her favorite pair of blue jeans, a white tee, and a green canvas jacket tied around her waist. "I had to pick up the sitter." She dropped her purse and car keys on the table, quickly brushing back a strand of her unruly, blond hair. "Isn't Bev here yet?"

"Nope, I'm all by myself," I said pretending to be hurt. "I'm sure she'll be here any minute.

"I need a coffee, bad," Julie mumbled as she searched for her wallet in her oversized handbag, which I was certain contained more than my bedroom dresser did. The door to the café opened again, and Bev strolled in looking rested and casual in Capri pants and a short-sleeved sweater. I always teased her that she reminded me of a black Diane Sawyer.

"Mornin' girls."

"Don't you look young and hip for a woman officially over the hill," I said referring to her big 5-0 birthday party last week.

This birthday was poignant. Bev had suffered a slight heart attack seven months earlier. To say we were shocked was an understatement. Bev was the picture of health with the only warning sign being an aunt and a cousin who had both suffered heart attacks before the age of fifty-five. We were all relieved that she seemed to have recovered completely with no lasting physical effects. She did seem more contemplative in the last few months, but I guessed that this was normal.

"Age is all in your mind, and I'm losing mine, so I will remain forever young," Bev chuckled as she and Julie headed up to the counter.

The three of us had been meeting regularly for years over a strong coffee and a firm bagel. We had all worked for the same company five years ago. A research firm downtown: decent money, good benefits, and generally low stress. We shared a cubicle and soon started sharing everything else: recipes, family photos, home remedies, advice, even the odd cold. Bev was the only one who was still there, and she never let Julie and me forget that; we had jumped ship and left her to fend for herself. I went to a large bank and began selling mortgages. The pay was better, but a cubicle is a cubicle. Julie left to have children, but was now facing a divorce and the unfortunate reality of being a single mom. She was feeling ready to get back to work, but we were trying to talk her out of returning to the firm and instead finishing her last two years of university to get her degree in business.

"Coffee truly is the last legal vice," Bev sighed as she took a satisfying drink from her cup of dark roast. "So, did you?" Bev asked.

"Did I what?" I replied.

"Type up your resignation, tie it to a rock, and lob it through your boss's window after packing up your paints, selling your house, and buying a one-way ticket to France?" Julie was joking, but she said it with enough seriousness to demand an answer.

The last time we met I'd promised that I was going to get my portfolio together and submit some of my work to a local art gallery that was accepting new pieces. I'm an artist, although I rarely call

2

myself that. For some reason it just sounds arrogant when I say it. Mostly, I just say that I paint a little. Downplay it. Maybe it's safer. People have fewer expectations of someone who does art as a hobby rather than one who boldly proclaims herself an "artist."

I also promised that I would approach my boss with the idea of a flexible work arrangement. Maybe I could work at home or do a job share or go to part time. I was beginning to realize that I needed more time to paint. A couple of things had happened in my life in the last few months to make me think that I should really start to take it more seriously. I had sold a few watercolors to friends of friends and visited an old art teacher who encouraged me to show more of my work. She also thought I should consider teaching at the local community center. The idea of having a reason to paint had a strange effect on me. I sort of panicked and stopped painting altogether for a few weeks. I, of course, blamed this on the unfortunate busyness of my life.

So three weeks had passed, but I had done neither of these things. I was kind of hoping that they had forgotten. But nothing gets by the girls.

"I meant to work on my portfolio this week, but I've been so busy at work ... I worked late almost every night this..."

"Blah, blah, blah." Julie cut me off. "I don't know about you, Bev, but these excuses are getting a little thin, don't ya think?"

"No, really. I've got three or four paintings that I need to get mounted, but the framing shop is always closed by the time I get there, and I've just been so busy..." I argued my case.

"Did you see Oprah on Tuesday?" Julie asked.

"Oh, yeah. Wasn't Dr. Phil talking about..."

"Ah ha! Oprah's on at four. The framing shop's open till six." My accuser smirked. "Busted."

I was treading water. "Would you believe that I taped it and watched it at nine?"

"Nope. Not for a second."

"I tried. I think I'll warm up my coffee," I stood, hoping to divert the conversation.

"Sit down, Picasso. I'm not done with you yet," Julie pointed at my chair.

I knew my friend was ready to launch into her sincere but

well-used speech on how bright my future looked if only I had more confidence in my abilities.

"Let me save you the trouble. I'm a chicken—a big chicken, I know. I hate my job. I'm sick of talking about it, and you're sick of hearing about it. I have a passion and a certain amount of talent and maybe even an opportunity to actually make a living doing what I love, but I'm paralyzed. I'm thirty-five years old with bills to pay and no husband to help with the mortgage. Is it really responsible for me to walk away from a regular paycheck? What if no one buys my stuff?"

"What if they do?" Bev piped up.

"Are you willing to live the rest of your life and never know?" said Julie.

"Well, when you put it that way, it sounds so final," I said.

"It is. You only go around once," said Julie.

"Unless of course, you're Shirley MacLaine," mumbled Bev into her cup. We all snickered.

"Okay, enough about me already. We'll come back to that topic, I promise, but what's going on with you?" I said looking at Julie.

"The papers came through last week. I guess that's it," Julie said suddenly looking quite tired. "The wedding was more complicated than the divorce."

Julie's marriage of just over eight years had recently come to a rather unassuming end. To most people it may have come as a bit of a shock to see this seemingly perfect family unit of a husband, wife, two children, and a cocker spaniel split apart. I, on the other hand, had watched the inevitable unfold for many years. Julie's husband, Mark, a middle manager at a growing tech company, had become increasingly distant, spending more and more time at his office. Julie did not respond well to this, and her rebuttal was to focus herself on their children and away from him. Their indifference towards each other did eventually turn into anger. The arguments that ensued, although never violent, were extremely hurtful. Having walked unsuspecting into a few of them, I couldn't imagine how the wounds would ever be healed from the pain they were inflicting on each other. At one point, after the dust had settled on a particularly harsh disagreement, Mark had insisted that they go to counseling. Julie disagreed. At first I thought she might have been in denial about just how bad things had gotten. Now I think it was simply her stubborn pride that wouldn't allow anyone else in to help fix the complicated mess of their marriage. She was never very good at asking for help, always believing that she had everything under control and that she would eventually be able to sort things out. This time she miscalculated just how much control she really did have over the situation. Mark lost his patience, and they both lost their tempers one too many times. In the end, their differences were simply irreconcilable. She was still profoundly angry but trying to get it under control for her children, if for no other reason.

"How are the kids?" I asked.

"As well as can be expected," Julie said taking a drink. "Mark has been good with them, spending lots of time, one on one, with them, letting them sleep over at his apartment. He'll have them every other weekend."

"How are you?" Bev asked.

"As good as can be expected," Julie half smiled. "Suppose I'm still in a bit of shock. This isn't how I ever imagined my life would be. Guess I'm still absorbing my new reality."

"You're still going to go back to school in September, right?" I asked confidently.

"I really don't know. Obviously when I made those plans I had a husband, a built-in income, and a free babysitter."

"You've had your heart set on this for two years!" I said.

"I know, but my life has taken an unexpected detour, and I don't know how I could possibly do it now, even part time," Julie sighed.

"There's got to be a way," said Bev. "You are too close to having your degree to walk away again."

"What with the lawyer's fees and everything, I just don't know how I could swing it now. Besides an old woman like me must be crazy to think I could keep up with those college kids. I'd probably need help carrying my books between classes!" Julie smiled.

"This from the woman who ran the Mother's Day marathon last year," I reminded her.

"A lot has happened since then. This just isn't the right time."

"It's never 'the right time,'" said Bev. "There's always

something trying to convince us to procrastinate a little longer: the kids are too young, we need to pay off the house, too old, too busy, basically just too scared."

"Listen to the sage," I mumbled somewhat sarcastically. "What's gotten into you all of a sudden?"

"Layoffs."

"What do you mean, 'layoffs'?" Julie asked.

Bev's eyes widened. "Layoffs. Four people in marketing, two in HR, and the accounting division was all but obliterated."

"Wow! That's harsh." I took a quick sip of coffee. "But what does that have to do with you? You're not nervous about your position, are you?"

"Shouldn't I be?" Bev said, asking the obvious. "Maybe it's only a matter of time."

Julie jumped in. "Come on, Bev, you've made it through dozens of layoffs. You know how it is; they let a bunch of people go and two months later end up hiring half of them back on contract."

I added quickly, "You've been there too long, you're too valuable. I'm sure you're safe."

"Maybe," Bev sighed. "Just the same, maybe I should start considering all my options."

"Such as?" Julie asked.

"Early retirement," Bev looked up from her mug.

"What?" Julie and I said almost simultaneously.

"Retiring. You've heard of retiring. It's what people do after working most of their lives. It usually entails sleeping in, some traveling, and an exorbitant amount of golf," Bev said rather matter-of-factly.

"I'm clear on the concept, Bev, but that's what *old people* do, people with gray hair who own sensible shoes. Not you," I said looking for an explanation.

"Well, I've had a little change of priorities over the last year," she paused.

We nodded knowingly.

"I'm beginning to think that work shouldn't be the center of my universe, anymore," she continued. "I'm hoping it won't take another life-is-short lesson to slow me down. I want to enjoy life while I'm healthy, while Gord's healthy. I'm not trying to sound morbid, I

just think I've had my wake-up call and should consider answering it."
The seriousness of what she was saying was not lost on us.
"I looked into the early retirement packages at work." Bev half-smiled. "They're not too bad. Gord wants me to do it. The kids are gone. The house is paid off. The job's okay, but my heart's just not in it anymore."

"So, you can really afford it?" said Julie jealously.

"Gord and I sat down last week and figured out how much I spend on parking and eating out for lunches and dry cleaning every month. Ouch! But it isn't just the money. We want to travel more, maybe finish some of the renovations on the house we've talked about for years, spend time with friends and family. We both agreed that it's time to start living the life we've been talking about for the last twenty years."

"You sound pretty convinced that you're going to do it," I said.

"It depends on the day, Sam. There's so much to consider, over and above the financial side of things. What will I do with all my time? Will I miss the social aspect of my job? How will I stay productive? And after I took four weeks off at Christmas, I was honestly feeling a little stir crazy in the house, not to mention that it got to the point that my dear, sweet husband was really starting to get on my nerves. Now that he works at home two or three days a week he is always under foot. Love him, but spending so much time with him is stretching the relationship—for both of us. It's a lot to think about, but hopefully I won't have to make that decision for a while. Someday we'll have that life we've always wanted. Which brings us back to you, Samantha."

"I had hoped we'd given up on that topic of conversation. Something about beating a dead horse," I said.

"No such luck. Why don't we type up our letters of resignation together?"

"Right, Bev. Have you forgotten that you still have this thing called a second income coming in compliments of your husband, Gord? Something I do not have," I reminded her.

"Like I said, there's never a good time," smiled Bev. "Besides, I'm nervous, too. It would be a huge life change for me. What if I get bored? Or lazy? Or reclusive? Or start taking in stray cats and start talking to myself?"

"That I'd like to see," I said.

"You know what we need?" Julie piped up.

"Besides rich, younger men who will cater to our every need and die before we do, leaving us independently wealthy? No offense to your Gord," I glanced at Bev.

"Yes, besides that. We need a Life Coach," said Julie.

"A what?" Bev said crinkling her forehead.

"A Life Coach?" I questioned. "You mean like a cheer-leader?"

"Sort of," said Julie. "Last week I bumped into this girl I went to school with, Nicole. We chatted for a few minutes and, of course, I asked what she's doing now, and she says she's a Life Coach. I gave her the same blank stare that you gave me, and then she proceeded to tell me what that is exactly. Wait a minute, I think I still have the card she gave me." Julie reached for her purse and began unceremoniously dumping its contents onto the small table. "Here we go," she said, miraculously fishing the business card out of the pile of lipsticks, loose change, Cheerios, and Kleenex. "It says 'Nicole Carpenter—A Life Coach for Life Change.' Sounds like what we need—a little guidance—someone to help us navigate through the these tough decisions we're facing."

"Someone to give us the proverbial kick in the butt," I said.

"You think I should call her? Maybe she'll give us a group rate," Julie said, staring at her card.

"I'm in. I could use some wise counsel right now. You?" Bev said, looking at me.

"Yeah, I guess."

"I'll call her right now, before we chicken out. To life change!" Julie raised her mug with one hand while digging for her cell phone with the other.

With the collective clink of our glasses and the sound of Julie punching buttons on her phone, the deal was sealed.

WORKBOOK:

If you could dare to tell that deep-down secret of what you have wished for in your career or retirement life, what would it be? More leisure time? Something you actually like doing? A sense of fulfillment? Travel?

What would your life be like if you had that? How fabulous? Be specific. For example, being 'happy' isn't defined enough. Instead write down adjectives that would describe you being happy—feeling good, laughing, enjoying your task, having a sense of accomplishment, etc. Perhaps you would like to pay the bills easily. Once defined, it becomes easier to recognize when you have arrived!

What is in your way? Or, do you get in your own way? Pretend you are giving advice to a friend. It is always easiest to say it to others. Now, do it for yourself. Example: Sam is concerned about finances. She needs to set up a budget and savings plan as a first step towards her goal. Need discipline? Do this with a coach or a friend to make you accountable to your own goals.

If you are considering retirement, what steps must you take to be ready for it? Bev is financially ready for retirement but not emotionally ready. Perhaps you are anxious about what others will think if you retire, or what you will do with all of your time. Maybe you will feel unsettled or strange not going to work each day! Identify what you need to do in order to 'feel' ready. Do you need to have a plan? Begin a new hobby? By continuing these exercises, you will be on your way to being ready.

If you have been the casualty of recent downsizing or are looking for a different career, what type of career/job would you most like? Think back to your childhood fun or a dream job. Consider, if success was guaranteed what job would you choose? What would your ideal work day be? If you are not sure, read on.

Regardless of whether you are retiring or are in a career transition, write down what satisfies you or dissatisfies you at work. This will assist you in knowing the components or tasks that you like or don't like, so that you can pick your next job wisely with that in mind. Likewise, the same approach may be taken toward your retirement. Sam knows she likes creativity, a steady income, friendships, problem solving, and contributing towards a goal. She dislikes routine and 'being in a box.' Notice, as you think about this, what could be added to your ideal day above.

Knowing this is key to being happy in your next job or in retirement. Want some help? Think back to some of your highlights at work. What did you find fulfilling in your job? Was it...?

a. Teamwork
b. Accomplishments
c. Friends/Community
d. Fun/Joy
e. Leadership
f. Learning
g. Challenge
h. Skills/Abilities
i. Routine/Structure
j. Tasks/Roles/Duties
k. Money
l. Feeling productive/Contributing
m. Decision making/Being in charge
n. Going out for lunch/Social activities
o. New opportunities
p. Helping others
q. Time away from home
r. Being a part of something bigger than you
s. Your company/Product
t. Working towards a mission/Goal
u. Having a purpose

Check off which ones apply to you. Then next to each of these write how you can find that same fulfillment in retirement or your next job. Commit yourself to doing or researching at least one item on the list. Identify any obstacles in the way.

Prepare yourself for your typical roadblocks. We all know our weaknesses.

Choose now to do something about any obstacles that may come your way.

What are some of your anticipated roadblocks?

What are some possible solutions to these roadblocks?

Bev's roadblocks are her anxiety of time spent in the house with her husband, staying productive and loss of social contact. What suggestions would you have for Bev?

Is this getting hard? Consider this:

We all know people like this: One person is enjoying retirement—she is active, happy, spending time exactly as she chooses. Another is bored, restless, and complains. The first has spent some time in thought, planning, and experimenting with ideas for a retirement that would be enjoyable for her. The latter has left it to chance, figuring he would deal with it when he had to. The problem with that is that most hobbies, friends, and activities are cultivated well before the retirement party.

Have you ever noticed the difference between some people who are between jobs, fretting and worrying about getting the next one versus others who are confident and who can define their skills and abilities and know it is just a matter of time before something becomes available? What is the difference? One knows their skills, talents, and preferences, and the other does not.

What if it wasn't as difficult as you think? I've heard countless stories of people who have set a goal, took steps toward it, only to find that the doors of opportunity present themselves. What is the difference between people? Preparation.
Completing these exercises will help you become happy in retirement or work.

CHAPTER TWO

Two weeks had passed since our unanimous decision to hire our very own Life Coach, and I was eagerly anticipating this first meeting with Nicole. It was probably a year since I had really started thinking about my life, my work, and my art. I saw myself gradually turning into someone that I didn't recognize. I was tired all the time with one uninterrupted, dull headache making me low on creativity and generally unhappy. This was not the life I had imagined, and I was not getting any younger. I needed to do something drastic, and just maybe this Life Coach was "the thing." Admittedly, though, I was a little nervous, too. I was hoping this wasn't going to be too much like therapy or that Nicole wasn't an ex-aerobic instructor looking for another way to get out her abnormal amount of energy. I needed motivation, but I was not ready for a Tony Robbins/Richard Simmons hybrid! As I pulled up to the café I smiled at the thought of all of us in our spandex and sweatbands doing deep knee-bends and reciting positive affirmations to ourselves. Yikes!

"Good morning, girls."

"Good morning, Sam." Bev and Julie looked up at me as I paused only briefly to remove my coat and then head up to the counter to order. I let my mind wander as I waited for Tony, our usual server, who was working his way through college, to steam the skim milk for my large latté. I thought again about what I was getting myself into. As much as I didn't like where I was, I was nervous about where I might be going. I had lived my life quietly harboring my dreams, safely enjoying my fantasies. The thought of having to speak them out loud and possibly start trying to turn them into reality unnerved me more than I wanted to admit. I felt the anxiety start to rise in the back of my throat. I was snapped back into the present with Tony setting my very full mug on the counter. I pushed a five-dollar bill across to him and dropped some loose change into the tip jar.

"Thanks, ma'am," he smiled looking up at me.

Ma'am? I couldn't overanalyze that too much. Instead I slid

my sunglasses off my face and pushed them on to my head. Grabbing my mug and giving him my attempt at a flirtatious smile, I tried my best to look young enough to be his girlfriend. I strode confidently towards our table.

"What's up ladies?" I tried not to look too obvious as I glanced over my shoulder to see if Tony had watched me walk away.

"You sound chipper this morning," Bev said.

"Yeah and you're not even caffeinated yet," joked Julie.

" I don't need artificial stimulants to be happy ... all the time," I said as I sat down.

"So are you ready for this?" Bev said looking at both of us.

I just started to answer when Julie said, "Well, you'd better be, here she comes."

The bell on the door rattled as a tall brunette with wire-rim glasses and a jean jacket strolled confidently into the café and directly over to our table.

"Nicole, how are you?" said Julie, standing to greet her.

"Sorry if I'm late and dying for coffee, but other than that pretty good."

"I like her already," I said in a loud whisper to no one in particular.

"Let me introduce you," Julie said looking towards me. "This is Sam."

"The artist," Nicole added.

"Wannabe," I laughed. "Nice to meet you, Nicole."

"And this is Bev."

"Contemplating retirement, right?" Nicole asked.

"Just contemplating." Bev held out her hand. "I know I don't look a day over twenty-one, but you'll have to trust me when I tell you that I've put in my time with the daily grind. Pleased to meet you."

"Let me grab some java and we'll get started, okay," Nicole nodded and headed towards the counter.

"Wow. No rest for the wicked, I guess."

"And no one's wickeder than you, Sam," Bev smirked over her large, ceramic coffee cup.

"Play nice girls. I don't want to have to separate you two," Julie said sternly.

16

"So you used to go to school with our Julie, did you?" Bev asked Nicole even before she had a chance sit down.

"Yeah, we met our first semester of university, in an art history class, I think."

"You took an art history class?" I said to Julie, genuinely surprised.

"Yup. It was an option. If I remember correctly I squeezed by with a sixty-six per cent, so don't ask me the difference between a Manet and a Monet," Julie and Nicole both laughed.

"We hung out for two years, but after Julie left we sort of lost touch. That's why it was so great when we bumped into each other at the mall. I'm looking forward to meeting your kids." Nicole smiled at Julie.

"Careful. If they like you, you'll make it onto the babysitting list," said Julie.

"I'll take my chances. So should we get down to business?" Nicole looked around the table.

We all nodded.

"Great. As you know, Julie gave me just a little background on each of you over the phone and I look forward to getting to know each of you better throughout our time together." She sipped her coffee. "Just to let you know where I'm coming from, I have a B.A. in psychology and almost eight years of corporate experience doing everything from training to marketing to recruiting. I think I've always been a Life Coach, of sorts, motivating people, challenging them. But I broke out and started doing this formally about four years ago. Now I work with people who have been laid off from their jobs, people looking at retirement, or people contemplating changing careers and so on—basically anyone looking at making a life change and aren't sure how to begin or they've begun and now need some clear life strategies to keep going."

"I think that covers all of us," said Julie.

"Great. Just to clarify, I'm not your therapist or your mother. I just hope to be a support and provide you with a little guidance on your journey."

"My mother will be glad she's not being replaced," said Julie.

"My therapist will be, too. I think I'm almost done paying off his new car," I smirked.

Everyone smiled and nodded knowingly.

"Okay, I realize that all of you are facing different challenges—from retirement to possible career changes and life transitions—but let me tell you that the principles we'll be using are the same for each of those scenarios. These principles are a series of questions and exercises that help you explore what you really want and how to get you there. It is customized to your situation because, through our discussions and the insights gained, you can create the job or life you like." Nicole looked at Bev. "Now Julie mentioned that you have already given some serious thought to early retirement."

"I'm not sure just how serious, but, yes, the thought's crossed my mind. I guess I'm nervous."

"What kinds of things are you nervous about?" Nicole asked.

"Number one, I want to make sure that I'm not making a rash decision based on recent events in my life," Bev said with genuine concern.

"You mean your heart attack," Nicole clarified.

Julie jumped in. "I hope you don't mind. I gave Nicole a little background on all of us so she would have an idea about where we were coming from."

Bev reassured her. "No problem. I don't mind." She looked back over to Nicole. "My husband, Gord, and I, have figured out the financial side of things, so that's not a huge concern," Bev paused gathering her list. "It sounds strange because the reason you retire is to get away from work, but I'm a little concerned that I'll get bored or lazy. I've always worked outside the home. Even when my kids were young I had a part-time job. I'm independent and very social, and my job has been a big part of filling those needs for me." Bev lowered her voice to a loud whisper. "My husband and I are also a little afraid that we might kill each other if left alone in the house for too many consecutive days!"

We all snickered.

"These are all very understandable, valid concerns, Bev, how could you plan for this? For example, how would you fill your social needs in retirement? What can you and Gord both do to ensure you continue to enjoy each other's company?"

Bev thought for a moment. "Absence makes the heart grow fonder, so we'll have to have some time apart and I'll definitely need the house to myself once in a while!"

Nicole reached for a large binder. "Good start! Keep thinking about it and jot down more ideas. In fact, I'd encourage all of you to begin a notebook or journal to record your ideas and progress. A good beginning for all of you is to create a snapshot of who you are. Who are you outside of your job, career, school."

"Who am I...?" Bev said with her voice trailing off.

"That's right up there with 'Why are we here?' and 'What's the meaning of life?'" Julie stated somewhat apprehensively.

"A little heavy for a Saturday morning, don't you think?" I looked for agreement from the girls.

"Don't panic. I'm going to help get you started answering this question, and it will also be part of your homework for next week," Julie said calmly.

"Homework? You're kidding me, right?" I piped in. "I hardly have enough hours in the day as it is."

Julie jumped in. "We all agreed to do this, right? And we all said that this could potentially change our life direction, so it's important, right? So we all make time for what we label as a priority in our lives. Let's label this as a top priority right now. We're either one hundred per cent in, or we're out. Girls, are you with me?" Julie reached under the table and pinched my leg while giving me a sideways smile.

Bev and I both nodded enthusiastically after our pep talk.

"Wow! Thanks. I should hire you to come on my first call with all my new clients." Nicole patted Julie on the back.

"No problem. Carry on, " Julie straightened up in her chair and tried to look important.

"Like the captain said, let's carry on. Here's a list of some components of what makes each of us unique, and then you can touch briefly on each of them. Don't worry about writing them down; they'll be in your handouts. Your *homework*," Nicole said gently. "When you can identify and define yourself and the components of your life, it makes life easier. You know who you are, what you want, and what is important to you. It makes decision-making so much clearer, which is especially important right now. These concepts are the foundation to all the rest of the work that we will do together, so it's important to spend some time here."

"Bring it on," I said in my most positive voice.

"So, they are Values, Talents/Skills, Community, Family/Friends, Vision, Standards, Self-Esteem, and Accomplishments. Also, we'll touch on Leisure Time and Spirituality."

"That's a long list," said Bev trying to absorb them all.

"So what are Values?" Nicole asked rhetorically. "They describe core aspects of you that make you feel most like yourself. When you are living and really *being* your values, you feel a sense of excitement, a connection and resonance as you go about your activities authentically."

"So when I'm painting, or 'in-the-zone,' as I call it, and lose all track of time, that would be a Value?" I interjected.

"Exactly. So you would say that one of your Values is creativity, or the act of creating. For someone else it may be when they are learning something new or when they are showing compassion towards someone. For me, one of my highest values is educating or motivating people. It's when I feel truly alive," Nicole said almost beaming. "Values enable us to articulate ourselves and what we stand for. When you are unclear about something, knowing your values is a huge benefit."

"For example…" Julie asked.

"For example, if you value honesty and are presented with a situation that potentially compromises that value, the situation makes clear what you should do, based on your value. Most of us live our values almost unknowingly or by default. We often 'adopted' them from our childhood heroes, teachers, or family members. I want you to take some time to discover your own."

"Got it," Julie said confidently.

"Next, we've got Talent or Skills; this may be what people compliment you on or what you most enjoy doing. Examples are supporting, negotiating, speaking, writing, and problem-solving. A talent could be something you have been born with, whereas a skill is something you have learned. Don't worry so much about semantics, just create a list. This comes in handy later on as you further refine your choices for career or retirement direction. It's a good idea to list what you think are each other's skills. Our perceptions of ourselves are often much different than how others see us."

"This could get interesting," I said leaning back in my chair.

"When you think about Community, ask yourself, who do you really enjoy spending time with? Are you involved with sports teams, professional associations, and volunteering? Which moves us into Friends and Family. What do they do for you; do they challenge you, make you laugh, support you?"

"Drive you to the brink of insanity." Julie smiled staring into her coffee cup.

"However you define them is fine," Nicole added. "And on to Image. If you consider that image precedes reality, then what do you want your reality to look like in three months? Five years? The importance of a clear, compelling, vivid picture of what you want your life to be cannot be underestimated. With that firmly in your mind you can't help but move away from what you don't want by moving toward what you do."

"I think we already agreed on the rich husband in failing health right?" I looked around the table.

"Maybe I need to give you some guidance around that," Nicole half-smiled at me.

"Ask yourself if you want a new career, what would it look like? What would it feel like? If you are retiring, what does that look like? You can look long term or on a day-to-day basis. Without a clear image we'll never get from where we are to where we want to be." Nicole paused a moment. "The next piece to our snapshot of ourselves is more action oriented; it is how we live our lives. We each have a code of behavior or standard that we hold ourselves to, such as being polite or on time. I would like you to think about this and write yours down."

"Interesting," Bev thought for a moment. "Yeah, I guess we do."

"Lastly," Nicole continued. "We know our Self-Esteem plays a huge role in our ability and willingness to make changes in our life, how resilient we are, and how good we feel! Going through life change can affect our self-esteem. This is a huge topic that you can read up on. Three easy ways to increase your self-esteem is by collecting evidence. Start keeping those wonderful notes, cards, or e-mails of acknowledgement others have sent you. The second is to create positive affirmations, and the third is to get rid of negative self-talk. Remember to write the affirmations as if they are already true. Use 'I am' statements. Now, use some of your gathered evidence and add to your list of accomplishments. This builds self-esteem and is good preparation for a job search, and the accomplishments can give you some ideas for spending time in retirement." Nicole paused and looked around the table. "That's it. The first step in discovering what a satisfying life could be for you. Congratulations on taking a big leap in an area not too many people do.

We all sat there looking a little overwhelmed as Nicole started handing out our homework for next week.

"I know it seems like a lot, but if we do this now, it will set the stage for everything else we do together," Nicole said encouragingly, "and set you up for success."

"I'm excited," said Julie.

"I'm glad. I am too," said Nicole. "And with that, I will leave this homework in your very capable hands and look forward to seeing you all next week."

"Till next week." I took a final sip from my lukewarm coffee and realized that my head was already spinning from all things we had talked about. I guess I'd never really given much thought to how connected each of the areas in our lives really were. It struck me that I was going to have to de-compartmentalize first and then try to figure out how to integrate everything together. I was going to have to look at myself in a radically different way than I ever had. I hoped I was up to the challenge.

WORKBOOK:

Help! Who am I?

Each of the following concepts is an aspect of you. By defining them, you will help to create a clearer picture of yourself, so that you can find a rewarding retirement or new career.

VALUES:
What do you value? About what will you not compromise? If someone described what you stood for, what would they say? Quickly write a values list now. Don't edit, just write every word that comes up. It could be a feeling, an activity, or a quality about yourself that makes you feel most comfortable and best describes you.

Values expansion exercise:
Have a friend or life partner ask you questions like "What is important to you *now* about your life?" or "When were you extremely motivated in your life, and what were you feeling?" Values motivate us, so know what motivates you.

Sam is motivated towards a painting career. She loves the feeling it gives her while she is painting. This is expressing her value of creativity. Julie values feeling good, so she expresses that by keeping in shape.

Ask yourself, what legacy do you want to leave? Our values can be revealed with this introspective question.

Number each item on your list in order of importance. Choose your top four and write them here.

* Start living your top four values*
Ask yourself … are your values being expressed in your life? Are you doing things now that aren't an expression of your values? What effect does this have on your life? What are you willing to do to change this? Feeling out of sorts could be an indication of a values conflict. Julie needs to identify her values to be able to make her decisions about her career easier. She is struggling because she has not identified them. Once identified, career paths can be further defined or narrowed down. In contrast, Sam knows she values creativity and a regular income. This is difficult because she is viewing them as being in conflict with each other. How do you think Sam could resolve this? How would you?

Still looking at your top four values:

List one way you like to express and live your values.
For example: If you value "being connected," you may regularly express that by writing letters to your out-of-town relatives or friends or by getting together with friends for coffee.

1)

2)

3)

4)

Some Examples of Values

Security	Refinement	Adventure
Speculation	Risk	Dare
Experiment	Exhilaration	The Unknown
Venture	Beauty	Elegance
Coach	Touch	Serve
Strengthen	Loveliness	Encourage
Contribute	Facilitate	Influence
Energize	Improve	Provide
Magnificence	Alter	Assist
Foster	To Catalyze	Create
Design	Invent	Impact
Synthesize	Ingenuity	Originality
Move Forward	Conceive	Plan
Build	Assemble	Discover
Perceive	Realize	Uncover
Distinguish	Observe	Emote
To Experience	Guide	Lead
Cause	Arouse	Rule
Persuade	Encourage	Model
To Feel Good	Be With	To Glow
Mastery	Adept	Best
Set Standards	Excellence	Pleasure
Have Fun	Be Entertained	To Relate
Be Connected	To Unite	Tenderness
To Nurture	Acquire	Touch
Be Present	Empathize	Support
Respond	Explain	Be Spiritual
Be Aware	Be Accepting	Prepare
Honoring	Educate	Instruct
Enlighten	Inform	To Win
Show Compassion	Attain	Be Passionate
Accomplish		

Values in action:

Example: Sam wants a career she enjoys because she is tired of just putting in time for a paycheck. She sought something that would motivate her so that she would be happy to get up in the morning and go to work. She looked at this list of words and circled her values and then identified her top four; Creativity and Mastery were two of them. With that came her "Ah Ha Moment," that, of course, she wasn't as happy in her current employment as she would be in a generalist position, which made it impossible to become proficient in one thing. Now Sam can make decisions easier and with more clarity by using this knowledge. It may take several months to complete, but, after all, Sam knew she wanted the thirty years or so left of work to be more rewarding than the past!

What words could you circle that would give you a similar "Ah Ha!" experience?

TALENTS/SKILLS:

What are you adept at, either at home or work? What do people compliment you on? What do you most enjoy doing?

Quickly write down as many talents/skills that you can think of. It is the person who can articulate their skills better that gets the job, not the one who is necessarily the most skilled. Knowing your skills is the first step to this ability, and it is also information for activities in retirement!

We can be described in three ways—who we think we are, who others think we are, and who we *really* are! What would others say are your talents or skills? Pretend you are an observant reporter watching you throughout your day. What skills would the reporter headline on the paper? If they interviewed your friends or family, what would they add to the article? Finally, what is your self-report?

Not sure what skills or traits to develop? Consider that today is your eightieth birthday party—what will they say about you? What do you want them to say? List it here.

Examples of Talents/Skills

Organization	Speaking	Writing
Leading	Cleaning	Communication
Calculating	Budgeting	Explaining
Resolving Conflict	Persuading	Negotiating
Interpersonal	Supporting	Team Player
Initiating	Respecting Differences	Directing
Decision Maker	Planning	Motor Coordination
Strength	Problem Solving	Analyzing
Researching	Synthesizing	Serving
Technical	Cooperating	Creative
Time Management	Fine Arts	

COMMUNITY:
Where do you really enjoy spending time? With whom do you enjoy spending time? What are you involved in—sports, family, professional associations, volunteering? This gives you ideas for potential jobs, networking, and activities in retirement. Sometimes our underlying passions are found here... Currently, Sam is ignoring this in her life, assuming her painting won't pay the bills. Too many of us discount something before we even try. Someone has to be the artist, dancer, or accountant! Why not you?

FRIENDS/FAMILY:
Do they support you, uplift you, challenge you, make you laugh? Do you enjoy being with them? Can you be completely yourself and real with them? Who are they...? List them. Include them as part of your transition process. Do you need to broaden your circle? How can you do that? One easy way is to take a class, or join an activity group.

IMAGE:
What do you or did you imagine your life or work to be? Make every day an image of choice, not chance. When you set a goal, and have a clear, compelling image it is more likely to happen. Spend five minutes in the morning envisioning your day, your goals. Soon it will become a habit. Image always precedes reality! Write down your vision or ideas for a GOOD day:

STANDARDS:
These are behaviors and actions you hold yourself accountable to. Paying bills on time, staying connected with loved ones, being polite are all examples of standards. What are yours...? What are the standards of your prospective employer? Boss? Are they the same as yours? Will it matter to you?

ACCOMPLISHMENTS:
Create a "Happy File" with testimonials, comments, accomplishments, cards, e-mails that you have received from people. This will also do wonders for your self-esteem!

Good work! You have done what few people bother to do. You can now answer the question "Who am I?" very well.

Are you like Julie? Are you not sure?

What do you love doing?
Take some time to really think about what you love doing. Experiment by trying new things. This gives you ideas for work or retirement. Pick up a Recreation & Continuing Education calendar. Try a pottery or dance class, learn to skate, take a course in history. Find a buddy who wants to try new things too. Take the time to discover what is fun for you. Fill a journal with all your new experiences and how you felt while you were doing them.

For research, you could always take contract work, be a temporary worker, job shadow, or even volunteer as a way of exploring different occupations, industries, and roles to assist you in further clarifying what you want.

CHAPTER THREE

I purposefully arrived at the coffee shop a few minutes early wanting some time to look over my notes from the past week before everyone else arrived. Already believing that I was fairly self-aware, I wasn't expecting too many surprises in my homework answers to the 'Who am I?' questions. And I wasn't, but there was something to actually writing down what was in my head and being able to see my thoughts on paper. I liked Nicole's suggestion that we start a journal, along with our homework questions, to track our thoughts and feelings throughout this process. I was never very good at journaling, though. I guess I had visions of it falling into the wrong hands and read aloud at my funeral. Nevertheless, I had trouble being completely honest with my 'Dear Diary' and, therefore, with myself. But I decided to throw caution to the wind and write down exactly how I was feeling and what was going through my head—the good, the bad, and the ugly. Now, rereading what I had written over this past week, I began to feel quite unsettled. Everything I saw on the paper did not match up with the life I was living. I really wanted to be painting, to be showing my work, to have a studio, to be traveling, maybe teaching, to have more control over my schedule. Instead, I was working long, structured days in a completely uncreative environment that was governed by deadlines and bottom lines. This was not the life that I had imagined for myself. Wait a minute. Maybe that was part of the problem. I hadn't ever sat down and really imagined what I wanted my life to look like, maybe because it just seemed unattainable, unrealistic. Maybe I thought if I never dreamed it I would never have to pursue it, and if it never happened I wouldn't be disappointed. Maybe...

"You look deep in thought, Sam." Julie sat down beside me.

"Just thinking about what I want," I said, looking up.

"What you really, really want?" Julie said, pulling out her homework.

"Yes, and why I don't have it."

Julie sighed. "I'm not sure that I'm totally clear on what I want, but I'm crystal clear on what I don't want." She paused. "I love my kids, but I need a reason to get out of the house, to feel productive. I don't want to be wholly defined as a mother, and I'm no longer a wife. I need to start doing things that are just for me, that I'm good at, or that I enjoy," she began digging through her purse for money for coffee. "I want my life to be different, but I'm afraid of change. I have an out-of-date résumé, a closet full of pants with elastic waists, and I don't remember the last time I left the house without spit-up on my left shoulder."

"You just need to build your confidence up again. Please tell me that you haven't completely given up on the idea of going back to school this fall."

"I haven't given up on the idea, I just don't see how I can make it happen now." Julie looked defeated. "Hey, did you talk to Bev yesterday?"

I nodded in the negative.

"She must have called me three or four times but never left a message. I saw her number on the call display."

Just then the door opened, and Bev slipped in and over to the table. I noticed immediately that something was wrong.

"It happened," she said with a sigh and then sat down.

"What?" I asked almost cautiously.

"What you both promised me never would," Bev looked wide-eyed.

There was a moment of silence as Julie and I struggled to imagine what it could be.

Then Julie suddenly grabbed Bev's arm. "No!"

"Yes," Bev said calmly.

"When?" asked Julie.

"Yesterday," Bev answered.

I finally realized what their monosyllabic conversation was about. "They laid you off?"

Bev nodded silently.

"Oh my gosh, I can't believe it," Julie shook her head.

"How are you?" I leaned in and touched Bev's hand.

"In shock, I guess." Bev said sounding very tired.

We all sat there for a moment not knowing what to say next. I felt a small, hard lump forming in my stomach. How could this happen? First the heart attack and now this. I was stunned and more than a little sad for my friend.

"What next? Did they offer you something? A package?" Julie leaned back in her chair.

Bev lowered her chin onto one of her fists. "They really didn't say too much yesterday. They just called me up to HR, thanked me for my years of service, said they were restructuring the department, told me I was officially being given my two weeks notice, and that I could enjoy those days at home."

"That's it?" said Julie incredulously.

"Oh, they said to expect an envelope to be delivered to my home in the next couple of days with more details," Bev thought for a moment. "Remember Doris from the fifth floor? Well, she was let go last year and was six years shy of retirement and they gave her a payout of sorts. I don't know all the details, but I think she got an okay bridge to retirement."

"Well, that's good," I smiled. "I'm sure they'll do that for you then."

"I guess," Bev half-smiled. "I suppose I'll have to wait till I see what's in the envelope."

"Good morning, ladies. How is everyone this morning?" Nicole had slipped into the coffee shop without our noticing. "You look like you're in an intense conversation."

Everyone looked up at her, but no one spoke.

Finally Bev said, "I was laid off yesterday."

"No! You're kidding." Nicole quickly sat down next to Bev.

Bev took a deep breath in. "I wish I was."

Nicole looked genuinely surprised. "I'm all about life change, but this is a huge life change—a bit of a shocker. How are you doing?"

"I'm not really sure. I'm just numb," Bev said.

"And I imagine you will be for some time," Nicole set her bag down. "Well, this will definitely take our conversation in a new direction."

"I don't want today to revolve around me," Bev piped up. "Really. Let's just carry on, and I'll just try to absorb whatever I can in my stupor. I think I just need some things to sink in, and then we'll spend some time on me."

"You're sure?" asked Nicole.

Bev nodded affirmatively.

"Okay, fair enough," Nicole pulled her binder out of her bag. "We'll move forward and then spend some time at the end letting you vent, if you feel like it."

"I'm sure I will." Bev smiled.

"Okay, so other than that bombshell, what else is new? How are you two feeling?" Nicole looked at Julie and me.

"Well, we were talking about how far apart our reality is from our dreams," I said.

"To be perfectly honest, bombshell aside, we were already a little depressed this morning." Julie said.

"Yeah, your homework is bringing us down," I joined in.

"Hmmm, should prove for interesting conversation this morning." Nicole stood up. "Does everyone already have coffee?"

"Nope, I'll join you." Julie popped up.

"Me, too," followed Bev.

Deep down I knew this was good for me, to be asking the hard questions, to be shaking up my status quo, but right now I was just downright grumpy. On top of that, now I felt guilty for feeling grumpy. Bev's life was going through a major shakeup, and I was worried about selling a painting and complaining about a job I didn't like. At least I had a job.

"Well, it sounds like you've all had a *good* week of self-exploration. Or at least a week of self-exploration," Nicole said setting down her mug and glancing at Bev.

"I'm sure all the homework you gave us is part of some bigger picture, but so far all it's done for me is made me more depressed than before we started." Julie nodded with me in agreement.

"How so?" said Nicole.

"Well, it's just shown me again how far apart my ideal self is from my real self. So much of what I think is important or that I love doing is not incorporated into my daily life." My frustration was showing through.

"What about you, Julie? Do you agree with Sam?"

"Definitely. I'm beginning to get a picture of how I'd like my life to look, but I just don't know how to get there. There are just too many obstacles."

"There's just never a good time," Bev said jokingly. "Man, those words are coming back to haunt me."

"I know it's too fresh now, but this really is an exciting thing, Bev. This adds a great new dimension to our group. We will actually have someone going through a radical life change right here in our midst a little sooner than expected," Nicole said with cautious optimism. "Not that that let's you other two off the hook. I'm expecting big things from all of you."

"We'll try not to let you down." I leaned over and clinked Julie's mug with my own.

"With that in mind, we should get right into it." Nicole glanced down into her binder. "We'll start today by talking about confidence. When you've had it in the past and why you may not have it in certain areas now. Each of you needs to ask the question why you are feeling how you are feeling now. Perhaps you are not confident enough to change careers or directions."

"I've been asking myself that all week," I said looking into my coffee.

"Great! Now you need to listen to your answers. Maybe there are other things you need to do in order to be ready for the change. What financial or emotion needs do you have? And how will you know when you do have confidence? Will you be able to recognize confidence when it appears in your life? What will it take for you to be confident and feel it?"

"I used to have more confidence than I do now. Not sure where it went," said Julie.

"You have to remember that you're still fresh out of a divorce, and that would wreck havoc on anyone's confidence," Bev was quick to add.

"Consider, that confidence is still inside you. Sometimes you just need to dust it off, so to speak. Shine it up. Think back to when you experienced confidence before. It came from inside of you. Before you can reactivate it within you, get a clear picture of how you felt the other times you experienced confidence. I want you all to do something right now. Close your eyes."

"Here? At the table?" Julie became immediately self-conscious.

"Yes. Don't worry. I won't hypnotize you and make you cluck like a chicken in the middle of the café," Nicole reassured us.

I took a deep breath and closed my eyes. Nicole had us remember a time when we felt *really* confident. It didn't matter where it was or what we were doing—maybe throwing an amazing dinner party, or doing a great presentation at work, or teaching something to a child. Then we went back to that time and relived the experience in the movie screen of our mind's eye, as though we were watching a movie from memory. She told us to go back into our body and recreate it and really feel the feelings of being totally confident. As we were reliving these feelings, when they hit their peak, we were supposed to squeeze our thumb and fingertip together and hold it for five seconds.

I thought back to the times I had spent teaching my thirteen-year-old niece how to paint, first with watercolor and then with acrylic. Although she obviously had some innate talent, it was her enthusiasm that really struck me. She was like a sponge, ready to soak in everything I was saying. Her huge, attentive eyes and eagerness to try anything I suggested made me want to be a better teacher. As the memory became real in my body I squeezed together my thumb and fingertip.

"After you've done this exercise a few times you will be able to just squeeze your fingers together and your body will respond by giving you feelings of confidence," Nicole said. "It's a sort of physical memory recall."

"Very cool, " Bev said looking down, squeezing and releasing her thumb and finger and enjoying her newfound power.

"This can be used for any positive emotion you'd like to recreate anytime," Nicole said, sipping her coffee.

"I guess I'm a bit like Julie," I said. "I don't think I lost my confidence because of one event, but it seems to be slipping away nonetheless. I guess I'm confident in things I know I can do or that don't have much risk of failure, but for the most part I am paralyzed by fear of trying anything new."

"Fear of failure can be just that—paralyzing," said Nicole, "and I don't want to downplay that fear. I've heard it said that there is no failure, only feedback. We may fail, but we need to realize that we are guaranteed failure if we never try. Failure is never attempting anything. We need to look directly at the failure and ask ourselves what's the worst that can happen if we do fail. If we look at the worse thing that could happen, ask yourself how could I *prevent* that from happening? And if for some reason I couldn't, could I live with it? And if the best thing happened, how would that make me feel?"

I added, "I guess people can't actually die of embarrassment."

"I came awfully close that day I walked across the entire third floor from the washroom to the staff lounge with half a roll of toilet paper stuck to the bottom of one of my pumps and trailing behind me." Bev covered her face with her hands.

"And we almost died of laughter!" Julie said remembering the day.

"Okay, so you may have *felt* like you were going to die, but you lived to tell and retell the story, much to our delight. Stemming from this fear of failure is often the fear of making the best choice," Nicole said moving on. "In your case, Sam, you have a sea of choices in front of you."

As I listened to Nicole I began to realize some of the choices I had. I could stay in my present career and continue to paint as a hobby. I could work part-time in my current job, or look for another one and pour more time and effort into my painting. I could decide to quit my job altogether and start showing my stuff at art galleries and maybe teaching a few classes. But were these realistic choices? I hesitated for a moment and then opened my mouth about to protest.

Nicole caught me and said, "I know you are about to say, 'What about my mortgage payments? What if no gallery takes my work? What if I never sell a painting?' Well, what if you *did* sell your paintings? How would that change the quality of your life?"

"Probably a lot," I replied.

"Make a choice. Even if later on you need to choose another path, at least you will know that you have eliminated one option! Most of us live our lives by accident, which is simply not making decisions and letting life, others, whoever, make them for us by default."

"I choose to think of this as fate." Julie leaned into the conversation.

"This is not fate," Nicole was quick to add. "This is avoiding making decisions, plans, or goals. When we don't know what decision to make, we don't make one!"

"Let me guess, you're going to say that by not making one, we're making one," Bev said knowingly.

"Exactly. By not making one, we've actually made one, and that defeats us!" Nicole said with growing enthusiasm. "Choose something! Anything! Try something, and if it doesn't work out, that's okay; move on to something else. Most of us remain stuck by not making a decision because we don't want to make a wrong decision. My question is, how will you ever know unless you choose?"

"Okay, I can understand this if you're buying a new dress and can't decide between the black one or the red one," said Julie, "but when it comes to the bigger decisions of your life, don't you think that's a little simplistic? If I get the red dress home and decide I liked the black one better, I just take it back and exchange it. But if I enroll in school or change careers and then decide I've made a mistake, it's a little more complicated. There's money involved and time and maybe even other people to consider, like my kids."

"I understand," Nicole said reassuringly, "and I'm not suggesting that you hop from job to job or make rash decisions when it comes to these bigger issues. I'm simply saying that, by using some introspection in your homework exercises and with our dialogue, you'll gain insights and knowledge of yourself—likes, dislikes, skills, etc. Then you are in a much better position to make a thoughtful, wise decision that works for you.

"Sometimes people spend more effort planning and researching their two-week holiday than they do their career and their lives! Give it careful planning and thought, and then *do it*. Let me give you an example from my own life. When I started college I was afraid of picking the wrong major. I knew it was a big decision, and I didn't want to mess it up. So I didn't make one because I thought it had to be perfect. And because I didn't know what was the perfect choice, I didn't make one at all. I sat down with a career counselor and he pointed out that not picking my major was just as imperfect a choice as making the *wrong* one. I gave myself permission to choose, realizing that there was no shame in the idea that I may choose something different down the road. What's the worst thing that could happen?"

"Well…" I started to answer.

"Rhetorical question." Bev punched me on the arm.

Nicole smiled and continued. "The worst thing might be learning something and taking a job that you eventually move on from. You still take the knowledge, skills, and business experience with you to the next job. And because you are doing your homework and exploring who you are, you will likely be close to making a good decision. Who knows? You might really like it for a long time, and, if not, you'll be in a better place to make another informed decision. If you don't like the job, you'll get another one. If you don't like retirement, you can go back to work. We need to redefine our concept of failure. Also, we need to realize that having the same job for thirty-five years, or even ten years, is not going to happen. So choose for the next few years, not the rest of your life."

"I like that idea," I said. "When I watch kids paint, they paint with no fear. They aren't thinking about whether or not their painting will be a success. They just pick every color that they think, in the moment, looks good and put it on the paper. If they don't like the end product, they just throw it aside and grab a fresh sheet of paper. I know that my fear of failure has prevented me from being as free an artist as I could be. So I suppose I could start thinking that same way in the rest of my life. If I try something that doesn't work out, just throw it aside and start a fresh sheet of paper."

"Beautiful!" said Nicole. "Another good thing to do is to ask why?"

"Why we chose what we chose?" asked Bev.

"Not so much that, but more so the whys of why," replied Nicole.

"You're going to have to elaborate on that one," said Bev.

"Gladly," said Nicole. "In your case, Bev, if you aren't experiencing this already, you may start to experience fears or anxiety around missing work, missing the people you saw every day, or feeling like you are contributing towards a team goal. When you start to feel this way, you need to ask yourself 'why.' For example, I will miss working. Why? I will miss the people. Why? I like to feel part of a team. Why? I value contributing. Why? Because I like to contribute. When you find repetition you may have found the answer. So, in this case, you may solve your fear of missing work by contributing with something else. Maybe you can be part of a team or volunteer."

"Got it," Bev said with authority.

"My head's feeling a bit full," Julie said squeezing her temples.

"We did cover a lot today. Thanks for plowing through it with me. Let me pull out your homework for next week," Nicole said snapping open her binder. "I just have a few exercises that I hope will reinforce what we've talked about here today, and remember to keep journaling—every day, if possible."

As Nicole passed our homework around the table, Julie leaned over to Bev and said, "Alright, girl, we need to talk. Just what are you going to do?"

Before Bev had time to respond Julie continued, "Are you scared? What does Gord say?"

As the conversation turned to Bev's impending decisions and possible new life my mind wandered through everything that we had just talked about—letting life happen to us, fear of failure, lack of confidence. I was so in control of other parts of my life—my health, my relationships, my time—but when it came to my career I felt that I wasn't an active participant. I got a paycheck every two weeks, regular promotions, and even the odd bit of recognition from my boss, but it was becoming clear that that wasn't enough anymore. I was becoming increasingly restless at work, but I couldn't imagine that I could do anything else. I had heard about people actually doing what they loved and making a living at it, but I guess I didn't think it would work for me. I couldn't wrap my head around a different looking Sam, outside of the nine to five and pantyhose. Thought comes before action, so I needed to change my thinking. I needed to see myself and my future differently. That's what I would reflect on this week—my perception of me and what was possible. I could be different. My life could be different. I was beginning to feel a bit like Dorothy from the "Wizard of Oz"—"There's no place like home, there's no place like home," click, click, click.

WORKBOOK:

Write down some areas in which you need motivation. It could be to continue the job search when you are tired of dead ends, overcoming rejection, to exercise regularly, or to finish that project (like your résumé or follow-up calls!) you started.

Let's increase our motivation!

Using the category of health and fitness, follow this exercise to increase your motivation in this area:
Close your eyes and picture yourself being motivated *now*. What do you look like? Feel like? What will you be able to accomplish? Think of all the benefits that being motivated will bring to your life. See in your mind's eye what this is for you. Close your eyes and think of the cover of your favorite book. Did you see it? Using this method, close your eyes and picture a time when you were motivated. Maybe you see yourself riding a bike or running. What are you saying to yourself? What are you feeling in your body? Do you hear anything around you? Can you smell anything? Take a moment to notice what is happening. See it in your mind, as you would while remembering and picturing your dream.

What are you noticing about your creation? Likely two types of picture will come up for you: one where you are reliving a great motivational moment for yourself, or one where you weren't and the picture was not quite clear for you.

If you are not as motivated as you want to be, enhance the picture if it is fuzzy or dark. Make it BIG and BRIGHT and right in front of you. If you saw it quite far away in your mind's eye (as a small dot on the horizon), bring it up close and right in front of your nose. What were you saying to yourself? Start saying encouraging words. If you didn't feel anything, imagine how good it feels right now, as you are motivated. Place that feeling somewhere in your body; maybe it's warm and spreading throughout your chest. Imagine a smell that may motivate you—fresh mountain air, for example. Do this now, with your eyes closed. You do not have to use all the senses, just notice which ones really make a difference for you. You'll know because all of a sudden you'll feel different, and more motivated! Often, size (big), color (bright), and location (right in front of your nose) are the keys.

You cannot do this mental exercise and not be more motivated. It works—every time. The key is to do it over and over again until you have 'sunk' in the message to yourself and your body. YOU CAN BE MORE MOTIVATED ANYTIME YOU WANT TO BE! First, choose to be; second, do the mental exercise.

The key to this exercise is identifying your current mental picture and altering it in a way that makes a difference to you. To remember the steps, just think of our senses—sight (big, bright), sounds (what you are saying to yourself, environment), taste, smells, and feelings. Or you can have someone read this to you slowly, step by step, while you create a new picture. Soon you'll be on your way to being more motivated!

Yeah, but how do I decide?

Choose a goal and write down all the things that could happen if you pursue it. What would be the best thing? What would be the worst? Rate them on a scale of −10 to +10, +10 being the best and −10 being the worst. Then ask yourself, what is the likelihood of the worst thing happening? If it did, could I live with it? Or, what can I do to ensure that the worst thing doesn't happen?

An example would be Julie's decision to return to university. Some of the things that could be going through her mind:

+10 *I am enjoying a successful new career*
+4 *I'm back at my old job after graduation*
0 *I graduate and have learned a lot about myself*
-4 *I don't like studying*
-7 *I run out of money or can't get find employment*
-10 *I fail out and do not graduate*

Now identify which are rational versus irrational fears. Now look at the realistic picture, which is never as bad as our imagination made it out to be.

Ask yourself, if these things happened would you still pursue your goal? How can you prevent the worst from happening?

Julie would likely say it is irrational to think she'll fail and not graduate. If money becomes a concern she could work part-time. In fact, after completing this exercise, Julie will likely commit herself diligently to her studies. Since she is now on her own, the investment and time she is putting in will likely motivate her to work very hard!

CHAPTER FOUR

I looked over at Matt, my boyfriend of almost eleven months. His dark hair was pushed carelessly under a baseball cap, and with his wrinkled t-shirt and track pants he looked much younger than his thirty-three years. We met at the wedding reception of mutual friends, and I was immediately taken in by his dry sense of humor and interesting travel stories. By our third date we also discovered that we shared a love of used books stores, Dr. Pepper, and old Broadway show tunes. Next to Julie, he was my biggest support and wisest critic.

"We're at the Crossroads," Matt pulled up to the curb.

"What?" I looked up.

"The Crossroads Café."

"Right," I looked up at the sign on the coffee shop we had been meeting at for months and only now saw the significance of the sign. "Yeah, I guess we are at the crossroads. Thanks for the lift this morning." I glanced over at him while he drummed his fingers on the steering wheel.

"No problem. Are you a little less stressed then last week?" he inquired.

"Yeah, I guess. For a fairly imaginative person, I'm not sure why I'm having such a hard time imagining my life differently. Like really different."

"Like without the regular nine to five?" Matt said a bit hesitantly. "Are you seriously thinking about quitting your job?"

"Maybe," I paused. "See? It's hard to imagine, right? But one of the things that Nicole said keeps coming back to me."

"What's that?"

"The whole idea that we'll never have a different future if we don't change the present. We all have this picture of our ideal future, which is usually quite different from what we're living right now, but we're too afraid to make any changes to get there. We get up every day, roll out of the same side of the bed, eat the same cereal, drive the same route to our job, do our same daily routine at work, come home, and watch the same TV shows, vacation in the same spot year after year ... and in our warped thinking we just assume that by doing the same things over and over someday, somehow, we'll get a different result. It's crazy."

"Makes sense," Matt agreed as he fidgeted with the keys dangling from the ignition. "It's just that quitting your job seems a little extreme, don't you think?"

"Maybe, but I have to do something."

"You know that I totally support you and your painting." Matt put the car in park and turned towards me. "I think you're an amazing artist, but do you think you could actually pay the bills just doing that?"

"What? You mean you won't take me in and support me?" I said blinking my brown eyes at him.

"Honey, I can hardly support myself."

"Maybe if you didn't have such expense tastes in cars."

"And women." He leaned over and kissed me.

"Jules will drop me at home, so I'll call you later."

"Okay. Get in there and change your life!" he said nudging me out of the car.

"I'll try. Call you later, and stay out of trouble."

"I'll try," he smiled as he pulled away from the curb.

I pushed open the door to the café and glanced over to our usual table, noticing that I was the last to arrive.

"When are you going to marry that man, girlfriend?" Julie said pointing out the window.

"Can we focus on one life change at a time, please?" I set my bag down next to the last empty chair.

"Okay. I'm just warning you: I'm on the rebound," Julie cautioned me.

"Matt doesn't really go for blondes," I said, pushing my dark brown hair behind my ear.

"No problem—I'm not really a blonde."

We all burst into laughter.

"Let me grab some java," I grabbed my wallet and headed to the counter.

"I'll join you." Nicole hopped up. "So, how are you doing? You looked a little tense when you left last week."

"A little. You'll have to forgive me if I seem a little defensive." I paused to order my coffee. "I feel a bit like a teenager being scolded by her mother. I know I'm doing something wrong, but the truth hurts, and it's like I'm trying to resist doing what I know I should do right till the end. Not sure why. Maybe it's pride. Maybe I don't want to admit that I've been doing something wrong."

"'Wrong' seems a bit harsh. I'm not sure that your life is 'wrong,'" Nicole suggested.

"I don't think it always was," I said reaching for my change. "My job, my choices, they were fine for a time. They served a purpose, but my life has become unhealthy. Deep down, I realize that I'm not doing what I'd like to be doing. Although I'm not one hundred per cent sure what that is. It's all very confusing."

"Hmmm. I think maybe today we should spend some more time on finding clarity," Nicole said.

"I could use some more of that," said Julie as Nicole and I sat down at the table.

"Sam was just saying that her goal is still a little murky. How are the rest of you feeling?" Nicole sipped from her mug. "But first, Bev did you get the mystery envelope in the mail?"

"I did. It was full of corporate-speak," Bev said, sounding frustrated. "Lot's of 'pursuant to' and 'herein referred to as.' Once Gord and I muddled our way through it all I think the bottom line is pretty reasonable."

"Good," Nicole said.

"There are a couple of sticking points around vacation time that I still have coming to me, but, to be honest, I don't really feel like the rest is negotiable," said Bev.

"You could get a lawyer. I know a good one," Julie added.

"I could, but I'd rather not." Bev paused. "They just complicate things and drag out the inevitable. I just want to be treated fairly, and I'll go away quietly."

"How are you feeling? Where's your head?" asked Nicole.

"Gradually coming out of the shock, but still in a general state of disbelief," Bev said running her finger along the rim of her mug.

"But you were kind of thinking about early retirement already so…" Julie said to Bev trying to understand her reaction.

"On my own terms. In my own time. I didn't want it to end this way," Bev said strongly. "I always envisioned that Gord and I would make the decision and have six months or a year to get things in order, to make plans. Then I'd hint around at work and finally give them a date. They'd beg me to stay…" Bev smirked mischievously. "They'd plan a big retirement party, and I'd go out—I don't know—with a bang of sorts." She paused. "It wasn't supposed to be this way. Why me? I feel a bit betrayed by the company. After all I gave them, this is my reward."

"It's hard not to take it personally, but for your benefit, you can't," Nicole said comfortingly. "It's the climate of the world we now live in: downsizing, rightsizing, restructuring, reorganizing—it sounds like they're eliminating the position, not you."

"I know that in my head, but my heart is still a bit bruised," said Bev quietly.

"Understandably." Nicole touched her hand for a moment and then looked at Julie and me.

"How are things looking for you two?"

Julie leaned in. "Sam and I have been talking this week about how to change our thinking—our perceptions of ourselves. Easier said than done. When your life has been one way for so long, you can't even fathom it any other way." She paused thoughtfully. "Like being married for eight years and trying to imagine your life as a single parent. I never thought I could do it."

"But you are doing it. You are living this new reality," said Nicole.

"I am, and—don't get me wrong—it's difficult, and, given different circumstances, I'd still choose to be married, but I'm not, and I'm okay. I'm building a new reality."

"You are so right to be focusing on changing your thinking to change your life. There exists nothing either good or bad, but thinking makes it so. William James," Nicole said rather matter-of-factly. "You become what you think about most of the time. What you believe, with feeling, becomes your reality. You have to focus on what you want, not what you don't want."

"So, once we have an idea of what, in our lives, we are

dissatisfied with, we should start to think about how it could be instead of dwelling on the dissatisfaction?" asked Bev.

"Right. Let me read you something from a book called "Learned Optimism: How to Change Your Mind and Your Life." Nicole held up the well-worn book. "It's by Dr. Martin Seligman, and he found linkages between optimism and positive mental health and between pessimism and decreased life satisfaction."

"Makes sense," said Julie.

"He came up with a method to reframe our thought patterns, enabling us to lead happier lives and be more successful in work," Nicole folded the book open and leaned in. "His technique is called the A-B-C model. Basically, he says that we all encounter Adversity in our lives. We react by thinking about it, which develops into Beliefs. A-B, are you following me?"

"Got it," I spoke up.

"Often we are so habitual in our beliefs that we don't realize their Consequences. Beliefs are the direct causes of what we feel and how we live our lives." Nicole turned the page. "If our thinking patterns are pessimistic—'It's my fault'—or permanent—'It will always be like this'—and pervasive—'It's going to undermine every aspect of my life'—then the consequences can lead to unhappiness and depression. The alternative is to change personal, permanent, and pervasive explanatory style to one that is temporary, at this time, specific, to do with this situation, and external, someone or something else."

"Hmmm," Julie sighed pensively.

Nicole carried on. "An example of pessimistic thinking would be 'I'm not a good student, *personal*, because I always, *permanent*, get Cs, which will never allow me to get into graduate school, *pervasive*.' Instead, an optimistic framing of a disappointing mark would be 'Although I am disappointed that the professor marked my work so hard, *external*, on this paper, *specific*, I know I can do better next time, *temporary*, and I can still get into graduate school.' The resulting change in Belief will drastically change the Consequence."

"I like that." Julie looked as though she had had a small revelation.

"Another illustration of how adversity, belief, and

consequence are intertwined is this story I once heard during a presentation." Nicole stopped to sip from her cup. "A bus driver picked up a passenger one day, who dropped his tiny, folded dollar bill in the fare bin. At the end of the day when the bus driver unfolded the bill, he realized it was torn in half. The driver got annoyed that a passenger had cheated him out of a fare. The next day, as the bus driver approached a stop, he noticed the same man. As this man came into the bus, he again placed his tiny dollar bill in the fare bin. Fuming, the bus driver carried on with the rest of the day thinking about how he could prevent this guy from getting on his bus the next day. After all, he thought, no one rips me off! That night, the driver had a hard time sleeping because he kept thinking about this man. The next morning, the bus driver had his strategy all planned out. He decided that he would ask the man to unfold the dollar before he placed it into the bin. Then, the driver could throw the man, caught red-handed, off his bus for not paying his fare. The more the bus driver thought about this man, the angrier he got.

"So, the next morning when he drove to the bus stop, he had already worked himself up into a tremendous state of aggravation. When the man came into the bus and before the driver had a chance to say anything, the man gave him a five-dollar bill and said, 'Thank you for letting me come onto your bus this week. I have been out of a job and could not afford to pay the fare. Thank you for preserving my last ounce of self-esteem and by not embarrassing me for my lack of bus fare over these last few days. I am happy to have finally found a job and could not have done it without you taking me downtown each day.'

"I often think of this story when I forget about the consequences of my beliefs and how important it is to think about alternative ways of looking at any situation. Now, when events happen in my life or I have negative thoughts, I ask myself, does this thought have value or not? If it does not, I choose and decide to release it and let it go like letting a balloon out of my hand and watching it float away. Or sometimes I imagine the little, nasty thought as a gremlin on my shoulder and flick it off."

"Fun!" Julie laughed. "My kids would like that one."

"A good way to further clarify your next steps to a satisfying career choice or retirement is to write out your perfect day." Nicole closed the book and slid it back into her bag.

There was a moment of silence around the table as everyone let their minds wander off. I was already pushing my freshly pedicured toes into the warm sand as I pulled the small umbrella out of my tall, chilled drink and leaned back into the soft, canvas lounge chair glancing over the top of my sunglasses at the brilliant sunset over the Mediterranean as...

"And I don't mean your perfect day at the beach," Nicole snapped me back to the coffee shop.

"Oh," we all said looking a bit confused.

"I'm talking about your perfect day, including some form of work."

"Work?" Julie asked.

"Yes, your perfect work in your perfect day," Nicole looked over at Bev. "For the time being, let's assume that you are going to retire, so for you it might include a half day of volunteering for your favorite charity or babysitting your grandkids. As much as we all like the idea of sitting poolside for the rest of our lives, some of us need a purpose, a reason to get up."

"Getting up to go to the pool is reason enough for me," I smiled.

Nicole continued, "I want you to describe, in detail, all the elements of an ideal work day. What are you doing? What is your role? What tasks do you complete? What time do you get up? Where do you work? At home or in an office? And what does it looks like? Are you in leadership? Do you work in a team or by yourself? How much money do you make? Do you travel? What do you do with your evenings? Bev, you do this, too, except that you are describing your ideal retirement day. Let your imagination run with this."

"So, you don't want us to write about what a *possible* perfect day would be. Like, what is within our grasp, but our dream day," I asked.

"Right. Be true to yourself. Think about what you would do if you knew you'd be successful and had the financial backing. So, you may describe your day in your big, bright studio painting great works of art to sell at international galleries."

"Got it," I nodded.

"I've always loved working in my garden, and I've dreamed

about being a landscape artist."

"Really, Bev? I never knew you'd thought seriously about that. You *do* have a beautiful yard," I said.

"I'm not sure that I have ever seriously thought about it. Maybe I will have to now."

"Think you should," said Nicole. "Once you determine your ideal day, then we can create an action plan with timelines to start the process. For example, if Julie wanted to be in a certain business, she would map out the steps required to go back to school, acquire financial support, and find babysitting. It is amazing that what may seem a far-off goal can be quite achievable if broken down into smaller steps." Nicole searched our faces for assurance that we understood. "If you are wondering how you are going to have the energy to do all this, let's have a look at what irritates you. I'm talking about the seemingly innocent things you put up with, like the lost button that irritates you every time you put on a certain shirt. That is lost energy. Remember these are things within your control to do something about. Let's not solve the world's problems right now. List things like that last ten pounds you want to lose or the faucet in your bathroom that drips or organizing your closet chaos."

"What's this supposed to do?" Bev asked, genuinely confused.

"Give us energy!" said Nicole enthusiastically. 'When we pinpoint these irritants and decide to eliminate them, you'd be surprised at how liberating that can be. It's all about removing these energy drains. And when we do, we realize that we now have the energy to go after our goals."

"I like that idea." Julie was writing down her assignment in her notepad.

"This is a lot of *stuff*." I rolled my eyes. "And we're supposed to do this all in seven days?"

"Thanks for reminding me, Sam," Nicole said, closing her binder. "I can't meet next week. I had a prior commitment that I just couldn't reschedule. Sorry, ladies. So you have two full weeks to meditate upon these things." Nicole took on her guru voice. "Before we all take off, remember to keep writing in your journals. Bev, I know you have a lot of questions and concerns about your next move. Write them all down and we'll look at them next time."

"I can still catch a ride with you?" I looked at Julie.

"No problem. Am I dropping you at Matt's?" she smiled playfully.

"Are you kidding? You can't be trusted. You'll take me directly home," I said matter-of-factly.

"Party-pooper." Julie pouted and crossed her arms.

"Just protecting my assets," I looked suspiciously out of the corner of my eye at her.

"You bankers are all the same." Julie uncrossed her arms.

The conversation quickly digressed into the familiar topics of men, dream vacations, new movie releases, and where to buy the best shoes.

WORKBOOK:

Pretend you have been guaranteed one wish from the magic genie. You can create your ideal workday. What would you be doing? With whom? A team? By yourself? Inside? Outside? Leading? Following? What tasks? What purpose, goal, outcome? Are you planning, organizing, completing a task, or using a skill? What type of people are you with? Where are you? Is your day planned or flexible? Spend a few minutes just imaging that day that everyone dreams of—a totally free day where you have the ability to do whatever you choose. Go crazy with this one and be very vivid, compelling, and clear!

Sometimes it is easier to write the worst possible day. Do that, so that you can go to the opposite to describe a great day. Choose the method that works for you.

GIVE YOURSELF A BOOST!

When you eliminate what is bugging you, you will feel much better! Make a list of ten things that are irritating you right now. These are situations that you are putting up with, that are within your control, and that are constantly distracting you: the leaky tap, loose doorknob, etc.

1)   6)

2)   7)

3)   8)

4)   9)

5)   10)

Create a plan to eliminate two items a week until your list is gone.

Let's create a snapshot of what you have learned so far. What have you discovered? Spend a few moments jotting down your insights and thoughts that you have about your next career or retirement plans.

CHAPTER FIVE

"I can't believe you actually did it!"

"Did what?" Nicole said, dropping her binder on the table and sitting down.

"Sam actually went in and talked to her boss about the possibility of working part-time," Julie was almost more excited than I was.

"That's great. And?" Nicole asked.

"Well, he was surprisingly open to the discussion. We talked about flextime or flex-place or maybe a job-share, and he asked for a proposal. So I proposed that I work from home two days a week. I'll come into the office for one day and for any meetings that I need to attend and that I knock my hours down from forty to twenty-eight hours a week."

"And he accepted it?" asked Bev.

"Luckily for me, there was this lady from our south branch that was just coming back from a maternity leave, and she's willing to pick up my two days in the office doing the administrative stuff."

"So, when does it start? What does Matt think?" Julie grilled me.

"Easy now." I patted her hand. "It starts next week."

"Wow! That's quick," Nicole said, surprised.

"I know, but I figure that I needed to do it before I changed my mind."

"Speaking of which, what *did* change your mind?" asked Nicole. "This is a big step. And you seemed awfully skeptical, even two weeks ago. Am I right?"

"Yeah, I guess. It just hit me that I'm not getting any younger and that I didn't like the idea of life just hitting me, of not taking control over my destiny, so to speak. I'm thirty-five, and I have a few regrets, but I don't want to be fifty-five and have a multitude of them. So, if I want tomorrow to be different, I have to make changes today. I also spent some time asking myself the 'what's the worst that could happen?' question."

"And…" Julie leaned over to me.

"And the worst-case scenario is that I never sell a painting, can't make my mortgage payments, and end up as your golf caddy,"— I looked over at Bev—"and sleeping on your sofa." I looked at Julie.

"That's not so bad," Bev replied.

"Exactly, so that's why I'm doing it. I've gotta try."

"And the best-case scenario is that you become a world-class painter, making more money than you ever dreamed of. Imagine yourself successful," Nicole said.

"But success can mean something different for everyone, don't you think?" asked Julie.

"Yes, exactly," Nicole agreed, "so everyone needs to define success for themselves. You'll never know when you've 'arrived' if you never know the destination. Each of you should find people who have found success in similar life-paths to yours, those people who are happy in their career or retirement, and ask them what they did, or are doing, to make it successful. This is very exciting, Sam," said Nicole. "And it'll give us a new direction to take our discussions. For homework each of you should write down your definition of success. Again, be very descriptive."

Interestingly, I had had this very conversation with some other painter friends after a workshop we had done together. Because you can be a great artist and not make a lot of money, it can be hard to know when to slap the label of success on yourself. I remember hearing a wide spectrum of answers to the question of defining success. One friend defined success by simply being creative; another said success was the ability to consistently create pleasure in his life and to continually grow and evolve; another talked about success being the progressive realization of a worthy goal.

"Create your own definition," Nicole continued. "As you live your life according to your values, and that definition plus, discover what pleases you and then do it. Weave in any other elements that define success for you, and you will make conscious, mindful choices to enjoy the journey as you grow towards your goal. This lifestyle brings gratitude, and what you want in life comes towards you much more easily. How's everyone else? How was the homework?"

"It was good for me to write down what I thought I was good at or enjoyed," Julie piped up. "It really made me stop and think about what my dream is, or if I even have one. And if I have one, why am I not living it?"

"Maybe not everyone has a dream," I added. "I know a few people who seem to be happy but really don't have a passion for anything in particular—no firm goals, driving desires, or pursuits. They're happy to have a job that is moderately satisfying, that pays adequately, decent relationships, no problem children, a good hair stylist, and two weeks at their cabin every year."

"You've raised a good point," said Nicole as she flipped through her binder. "We may not always understand other people's dreams, or seeming lack of them, so it is important to live our lives the way we want and not project our vision or values on others. These differences are what make us unique and what makes us happy may not make another happy. That's how it should be. Why do you think people don't go for their dreams?"

We all stopped to think.

"They don't believe they can," I said. "Either they don't believe enough in the dream, or, in the case of a career, they don't believe that they could actually make any money doing it."

Nicole made a quick note on her paper. "Okay."

"They aren't exactly sure what to dream, what would satisfy them. They don't know what would bring them joy, so instead of starting down a path that may be wrong, they just stay put, doing nothing," Julie said confidently.

"Excellent," Nicole agreed.

"I know you think everyone has one," Bev looked at Nicole, "but maybe they're not convinced that they even have a dream, or it's just never been acknowledged."

Julie nodded her head. "I also think people are busy and don't want to add one more thing to their lives. They just don't have the time for a dream."

"Amen." I raised my mug.

"I absolutely agree." Nicole looked up from writing. "So when thinking about living your dream what do you need to eliminate before you begin to add more things."

"I think the word dream can be a bit too ethereal."

"Huh? Can you translate that Bev?" Julie looked confused.

"Abstract, intangible, ooey-gooey. People still believe hard work, meaningful or not, is the only way to succeed."

"I'm not against *hard* work, but if you want to put your heart and soul into something, make it meaningful to you. We all spend due diligence in pursuing our career of choice. I love Joseph Campbell's quote, 'Follow your bliss and you never work another day in your life.'" Nicole kept writing, "These are great, what else?"

"Fear," I piped up.

"Of?" asked Nicole.

"Of success, of rejection, of being different."

"Excellent, Sam."

"Laziness," Bev added.

Nicole looked up quickly. "The important thing is to know *your* reasons for not going for your dream and look at it, then decide what to do about it. I've heard so many people discount their dream before they've even researched it or looked for ways that it could happen. Yes, it may take time and some creativity. I worked a full-time job and went to school at night. When I decided to go to school full-time I had to figure out how to make the mortgage payments on my place by renting it out, living simply, and working part-time. When you really want something you can figure out how to make it happen. At least give it a go! People have told me how surprised they are that when they set their intentions doors start to open. They won't open sitting here. As far as the fear of success and failure, being different does play a part. People wonder how their lives will change, their friends' and family's reactions. I ask people the question, 'who's life are you living anyway?' Yours? Or your family's? Maybe they would support you—check. If not, how important is that to you? Remember that well-meaning advice may not be the best advice for you. Sometimes people even wonder if they can pull off their dream, and if they do, can they keep it up! Let's go back to what Sam said, that some people don't believe their dream is a financially viable idea. They perceive it to be too much pressure, so they won't bother to try. "This is probably the biggest obstacle I hear coming from people that are working in a job that is unsatisfying or just wrong for them.

They'll say that the work's not that bad, and at least they're getting paid a lot more than they could make doing something else," Nicole paused for effect. "I always ask them what they are paying for their 'good salaries.'"

"Hmmm…" I agreed with a sip of my coffee.

"Maybe they think that it's selfish to go for their dream," said Bev.

"You bet," Nicole continued. "We need to value ourselves enough to be self-*ish*. Being self-*ish* is about taking care of yourself first so that you can care for others even better. How can you really care for others if you don't care for yourself? It's like coming from a half-empty glass instead of a full one. You have less to give, and what you do give is half-hearted. Sometimes we ask, 'Why do I deserve to be happy when so many people are not? How can I spend so much time on myself when I have kids or a husband or whatever?' I suggest you do one thing a day that is just for you—a walk, a bath, a nap. Practice self-care and you'll actually be able to take care of others even more. Okay, one more reason why people don't go after their dreams?"

After a few moments of thought I added, "People are just not ready, not in the right head space or time in their life."

Nicole agreed. "I think people are aware that it requires a significant investment in themselves to get their lives turned around. It can be hard work that will take time and dedication. It could also be easier than you may think. Being self-*ish* and taking good care of yourself is a good reminder now for you, Bev, you may receive dozens of phone calls to baby-sit, volunteer, run errands for others because they think you have all the time in the world. It's a good idea to think about your response to these potential situations before they come up."

"Good point," Bev agreed.

"Speaking of which, I know that you signed off on all the details of your package from work, but in your last e-mail you were still kicking around the idea of looking for another job? Is that still your thinking?" Nicole said, taking off her glasses to clean them on a corner of her light cotton shirt.

"Well, I can't say that I am completely over the shock yet," Bev said, "and I'm a little concerned that I'm making this decision prematurely, but it looks like I'm going to take this opportunity to leap into retirement." She smiled. "It even feels weird just saying it."

"Congratulations, my friend." Julie and I both reached over and gave Bev's shoulder a squeeze.

"So, you've already had some time off. How does it feel?" asked Nicole.

"Just feels like I'm on vacation, so I'm not sure that it's really sunk in yet. I've started a few projects that I swore I'd get to 'some day,' like doing nice family photo albums for each of my kids, organizing my recipes, and taking a bunch of my old clothes to Goodwill."

"You'll let me know when you decide to part with any of your no-longer-needed work clothes, right?" asked Julie.

"Yeah, sure. Let me dry clean a few things, and then you can come over and have a look."

"So, you're already feeling pretty comfortable in your new life?" said Nicole.

"Yeah, for the most part, but, like I said, it still doesn't feel real yet," replied Bev. "I did have a weird experience just two nights ago, though. Gord and I had just finally made the decision that this is what I would do and we had gone to a barbecue at Gord's boss's place with staff and some clients. A couple of times during the evening I got the inevitable question, 'So, what do you do?' The first time, I was taken a little off guard. Guess I hadn't really thought about that, about what my answer would be. So I just said, I'm recently retired. You should've seen the looks I got. Talk about a conversation ender."

"Did it bother you to not have a job title to put behind your name?" Nicole asked.

"I suppose, a little. I just wasn't prepared for the blank stares after I said it. Maybe they were thinking I was too young to retire or that I couldn't possibly have anything to add to the conversation if I didn't have a career."

"Try saying you're a stay-at-home mom," Julie jumped in. "People just assume that you must sit at home eating pretzels, folding laundry, and watching soaps all day, so what could you possibly have to say that would be intelligent or relevant?"

"This is very common to people who retire, are in career transition, or stepped out of a usual job description maybe to raise children or become entrepreneurs or start a home-based business. Job titles provide us with a sense of identity and status for us." Nicole looked at Bev.

"I didn't think that I was defined by my job, but I suppose, to an extent, I was."

"How else can we define ourselves? Our work can be something that we are proud of, but it doesn't entirely define who we are. Remember, we identified that at the very beginning. We are much more than our work; we are our values, talents, part of a community, and so on. The only person that needs to approve or understand or *get* what you are doing is you. We care way too much about what others think and sacrifice our energy in the process."

"So, how should I answer the 'What do you do?' question?" asked Bev.

"'Kept woman' doesn't grab you?" I asked.

"I don't mind it, but Gord might object," laughed Bev.

"What do you think, Bev?" asked Nicole.

"I could start with 'retired,' then carry on to say that I am currently seeking a new life passion, or I am planning my travel itinerary, or I am catching up on thirty years of lost sleep and good books," said Bev.

"Great. Make it fun. Forget the 'expected' answer," Nicole smiled. "I recently met someone at a networking event who answered my question, 'What do you do?' with 'I'm currently waiting for my next opportunity.' I didn't understand right away that he was in career transition, so I asked what industry would he like his next opportunity to be in, and he said, 'I'm in the wireless industry seeking a position in a company where my sales skills and values would be a good fit for their company.' I was very impressed with his responses. Isn't that better than saying, 'I've been laid off'? I know of another person who experienced strange reactions when they said they retired because they did not look 'old enough' to retire. Interestingly enough, he felt frowned upon by others; they projected that it didn't make sense that he was retired. He tried various responses. One was 'volunteering,' and another was 'retired,' and a third was the 'stay-at-home dad.' It was only when he said he was going to school that he felt accepted by others. It's like people can't seem to come to terms with a different way of living."

"You know I'm dying to answer, 'I'm an artist,' to that question and try to keep a straight face," I said. "It doesn't even sound convincing to me, so how am I going to convince someone else?"

"Maybe once you start doing it more seriously, getting more immersed in it, it'll come more easily," said Nicole. "You have to convince yourself first before you'll convince anyone else."

"I'm sure it'll be rolling off your tongue in no time," added Julie.

"Just to build on the idea of being defined by your title," said Nicole, "it can also be easy to be defined by your paycheck."

"Or in my case, an alimony check," Julie smiled.

"I remember when I first decided to leave my normal, safe, nine-to-five job and be a Life Coach, it was quite an adjustment. I was surprised at how much of my self-esteem and identity came from my job and having a regular income." Nicole paused contemplatively sipping her coffee.

"But I'll bet you snapped out of that," Julie said, snapping her fingers.

"And I'll bet you're gonna tell us how," I said facetiously.

"Yes, I am," Nicole said, smiling confidently. "First, I redefined who I was outside of my job, just like we did at the very beginning. I realized that because I didn't have money coming in regularly that I felt that I wasn't deserving enough, or good enough, and that I wasn't contributing in the way I used to. I realized that it was not really valid to tie those two things together. I'm still making money, just not in as structured a way as before. No sense feeling bad about it. I also gave myself permission to dip into my savings and some of the severance package that I had received for a monthly income. I also sat down and thought about how much more I was than just my work. I am athletic, a great cook, bilingual, outgoing, personable, and confident."

"You are more than just your work," I joked.

"My list of maid, chief cook, and head car-pooler just doesn't sound as impressive as yours." Julie half-smiled.

"Those are great titles! Being a good mom is an awesome responsibility and something to be proud of," Nicole added quickly. "If it seems like a long time that you've been primarily a parent, think back to what you used to love to do in your spare time, back when you *had* spare time."

"Let me help get you started," I said, leaning over to Julie. "You are an amazing seamstress, you aren't too bad with a set of hair-cutting scissors, you make a mean mocha cheesecake, and you are the only one I know who completes the Sunday crossword puzzle every week."

"Thanks." Julie smiled at me.

"Is there more to your redefining story, Nicole?" asked Bev.

"A little," she replied. "I also made the transition from getting self-esteem from external sources, like my paycheck, to getting it from with me."

"Easier said than done," Bev added.

"Maybe. I started by looking at any unmet needs that I had."

"Aren't all needs unmet?" I said, trying not to sound sarcastic.

"Until we devise a way to get them met. A need is something Not Expressed Each Day that is not fulfilled within. It often drives our behavior until it is met. As an example, if you have a need to receive praise or acknowledgment as a means of maintaining or building your self-esteem, realize that you are giving away power and control in your life. You don't want someone else to provide you with your self-esteem or happiness. You already have it. It just gets lost through our negative self-talk or bad experiences or critical people. Choose to accept your opinion, not the opinion of others."

"But the opinion of some people in our lives has to be important, doesn't it?" Bev asked genuinely, "—like spouses or friends."

"Of course. It's human to look for affirmation from certain people. Be careful in choosing those people because you have to realize that you are giving them influence in how you feel," Nicole said.

I had to agree because depending on what others thought and said about me often determined my mood and my self-esteem of the day. I was beginning to see that I needed to value and validate myself. I had to begin using the tools I'd been given so far and realizing that the more I reminded myself that I was already a valuable human being the less influence others would have over me.

"Besides, others are clouded from their own unmet needs as

well. They will view your situation from that clouded perspective," Nicole carried on. "So, next, get your needs met once and for all. The fewer needs you have, the more satisfied you will be."

"Makes sense." Bev nodded.

"After realizing that needs are something that must be satisfied in order for you to be yourself, fully yourself, you will move forward. And this is the difficult part, especially for women. One way of getting a need met initially is to ask people to help meet that need."

"What a concept!" Julie laughed. "But is it possible?"

"Yes," said Nicole. "Ask specific people to help you on a specific need, until it is met. You'll see how much this can change your behavior and activities and after a while the need is met, and you don't need their help anymore. A good example is people who have a strong unmet need for acknowledgement, so they'll do all kinds of things to be acknowledged. This need drives their behavior, so they work long hours, volunteer, go above and beyond what is required just to get that one piece of acknowledgement. If they were being acknowledged regularly from people who meant something to them, at least for a period of time, the need would be getting met and they would have lots of new, healthy energy, not to mention extra time because they wouldn't be doing all sorts of things to get this need met."

"That's just weird—outright asking people to meet your needs." I squirmed in my seat.

"Again, choose wisely. I'm not saying that you should ask your new next-door neighbor to tell you you're beautiful every day or that your tennis coach needs to tell you how smart you are at every lesson. But the people you are closest to you in your life shouldn't have any problem affirming you, if they don't already. Sometimes you just need it to be more specific or more often." Nicole paused. "And it's not forever, just until you feel that that need has been sufficiently met as you will notice, because it will no longer drive your behavior."

"Hmmm…" I contemplated that idea.

"We've covered a lot again this morning, ladies, and I have to run," Nicole began closing up her binder. "You guys are doing great, really. Don't get frustrated if you don't think you see progress. I can see the small steps you are already taking just in the questions you are asking. I'll e-mail everyone with your homework for next week, and I look forward to hearing how your new work arrangement goes this week, Sam."

"Me, too." I smiled.

"Keep journaling?" asked Bev.

"Of course. Sorry to have to rush off. I'm sure I've given you lots to think about. Talk amongst yourselves and I'll see you all next week." Nicole stood and was out the door before we hardly had our farewells out.

WORKBOOK:

"The greatest discovery of my time was that human beings can alter their lives by altering their attitudes." – William James

"Thoughts are just thoughts, judging them is what makes them positive or negative. The color of our attitude shapes our reality. What colors do you see?" – Larry Wayne

Are you worried about the opinions of others? Sam is. She is worried about what her parents or friends will think when they find out she is giving up a 'perfectly' good job to do something 'crazy' like be an artist.

Is there anything getting in the way of you choosing a career path or considering retirement? Write this down.

Would it be better to put your value on your own success rather than valuing the opinions of others? When you truly approve of yourself, you won't need it from others.

SO, WHAT CAN YOU DO?

Play the 'why' game. For example:
Ask yourself, why am I so worried about others' approval? So that I will feel accepted. Why do I need to feel accepted? So that I am included. Why is that important? So that I feel good about myself. Why? Because I will feel bad if I'm not accepted by another. Why? I don't like to feel bad. Once answers repeat, ask yourself, do I really need to feel bad because one person doesn't approve? Is this really valid? We often exaggerate things in our mind, and when we stop and take a close look we realize they are not as bad as they seemed, or that the belief is no longer valid. Once you realize this, let it go and determine that it will never bother you again.

What did you come up with?

The more you choose to create your life as you like it and become happy with that, the less you are worried about what others think. By consistently making wise choices and decisions, living your values, raising your standards, experimenting with ways you can enjoy each day, the more carefree you will be!

WHAT DO YOU DO WHEN THEY ASK YOU WHAT YOU DO?

If you are retired, making a transition between careers or jobs, a student, a stay-at-home parent, think of how you can more accurately answer the question "What do you do?" Think about your hobbies, your talents, how you spend your time and where you spend your money. You may say that you are a gourmet cook with a love for Thai food, or that you have a love for interior decorating or are an avid fly fisherman. Find new ways to describe yourself. Try a few new titles on and see how they feel! Julie tried this one: "I'm currently seeking a new opportunity where I can use my skills in business analysis and marketing." If you know what industry you like to work in, add that to your sentence. Bev might say, "I'm taking early retirement so that I can volunteer and play all the time!"

Finish the sentence. "I'm a…

IS SOMETHING IN YOUR WAY? OH, MY ACHING N.E.E.D.

A n.e.e.d. is something Not Evident Each Day and that we must have in order to be our best. And when needs aren't met each day, we go out of our way to get them. You may need acceptance, praise, adoration, validation, comfort, power, balance, control, acknowledgement, safety, influence, a voice. You can get by without having these needs met, but for an effortless, rewarding, and successful life, n.e.e.d.s must be identified, addressed, and handled. Most of us spend our lives trying, consciously or not, to get these n.e.e.d.s met. At best, we treat the symptoms or get temporary relief from them. This is because we assume these n.e.e.d.s will 'always be with us' and 'that's just the way we are.' This is not true. It is possible to have all of your n.e.e.d.s permanently met and to free up more time in your life that was once spent chasing these n.e.e.d.s. Needs Not Evident Each Day deplete our energy. It's like trying to run a race dehydrated. N.e.e.d.s can be met, so you can be FREE! Drink up!

So you must identify what your personal needs are.

List your top five needs:

1)

2)

3)

4)

5)

Now choose two at a time to work on over a period of thirty to sixty days. For the two needs you are working on ask yourself these questions: "Why is this a need? Who am I when I get this need met? How do I act? What do I think about? What motivates me? Who am I when I don't get this need met? How do I behave? How do I feel about myself? About others? About life? How am I going to get this need met? What changes can I make in my life in order to fully meet and satisfy this need?" Give three specific and permanent changes that you can make for each need.

One easy way for Sam to meet her n.e.e.d. for acknowledgement is to include her friends by asking them to say or do specific things to help satisfy this need. People like to help! She could ask three friends to acknowledge her sincerely (we can always find something to acknowledge in others) every time they see her until she tells them not to. Eventually, she will move on to getting her n.e.e.d.s met within herself. Once met, they will no longer drive her behavior, and she will feel much, much better! And you will, too!

SUCCESS AND YOU

How will you know if your life or career is a success? A successful life may be defined as being creative, or the ability to consistently create pleasure or to grow and evolve. Create a definition of what success means to you, then you will be clear on when you have 'arrived' and can go about enjoying your days. Too often we go from goal to goal and never really enjoy the pleasure and satisfaction from obtaining it. This is what Bev has done and that is why she feels funny not having a purpose in retirement life.

CHAPTER SIX

It was already unusually warm by the time I arrived at the coffee shop, or maybe it was just that I was running a little late and had rushed to get there. Either way, I was hot and bothered. The past week I found myself agitated and more than once I'd blown up at a colleague or Matt. The initial enthusiasm of having to change my life had worn off, and now I was frustrated by not seeing results soon enough. I was mad that I had let myself believe that I could actually make my dreams realities. I didn't really want to be here this morning, but I took a breath and pushed open the door to see Nicole and Julie already deep into conversation.

"Morning, girls."

Julie looked up. "Morning, stranger. How come you didn't call me back last night?"

"Sorry, Matt and I were having a … discussion." I rolled my eyes.

"Oh. Who won?"

"Not sure. The jury is still out." I sat down. "He wants me to apply to teach at the community college *and* show some of my stuff at this art show next month *and* look into renting a studio."

"Aren't those all things you want to do?" Nicole asked.

"Yes, but that's not the point," I said defensively. "I want to do them all, eventually. Not tomorrow! I feel like he's pressuring me. He was totally supportive of my going to part-time with the job to pursue my art, but I feel like he wants to see results from my decision, like now. I'm still trying to just figure it all out, get my bearings."

"So it's not what he wants you to do, but how fast he thinks you should do it?" asked Nicole.

"Right."

"Have you kissed and made up, yet?" smiled Julie.

"No, but we're going out for dinner tonight, and he's letting me choose the restaurant, so I'll make him and his wallet good and sorry." I laughed.

"I hate to take sides," Nicole went back to the discussion, "but I would have to agree with Matt, to a point. In some way or another, you've waited your whole life for this, so I wouldn't wait much longer. You need to start taking definite action towards achieving your goals. So, what *did* you do this week to get you closer to living your perfect day?"

Just then the door swung open and Bev and Gord stepped in, smiling, and both looking younger than I felt.

"Don't worry, ladies, I won't interrupt your session. I wouldn't want to taint your discussion with my *narrow*, male point of view," said Gord as he approached sheepishly.

"Are you sure?" I joked. "We could probably use some testosterone to balance out our perspective on things."

Gord flexed his bicep trying to look as manly as possible and then reached out his hand to Nicole. "Hi, I'm Gord."

"Nicole. It's nice to finally meet the man behind the woman."

"Wait a minute. I thought she was the woman behind the man!" Gord shook his head.

"Tomato, tomahto," Bev chimed in.

"So to what do we owe the pleasure of your company this morning, sir?" Julie asked.

"Just dropping off my lovely wife on the way to taking her car in for an oil change and thought I needed some oil myself to start the day. Coffee, to go."

"Has your newly retired wife been finding things to fill her days, or has she been driving you crazy around the house?" asked Julie.

"Well, she has been under foot a little more..." Gord was interrupted abruptly by Bev punching his arm.

"I think I'll take the fifth on that and leave that topic of conversation up to the experts!" He turned to leave, then turned back around. "Nice seeing you all; nice to meet you, Nicole. Pick you up at 12:30." A quick kiss on Bev's cheek, and he slipped up to the counter.

"You gals looked like you were already in a good discussion

when I came in, do you need to finish it off while Bev and I get a coffee?" I stood.

"I was just feeling like I needed a little pre-session pep talk," Julie confessed. "I just don't feel like I'm making any progress. Bev retired and has this whole new exciting life of free time."

"It's not that exciting, yet," Bev interjected.

"Okay, but you're following your dream of becoming an artist." She looked at me. "I'm still just a single mom whose main source of income is alimony, child support, and any free Tupperware I get if I host a party."

"Go back to school," I said too quickly. "Sorry. I just think you have a solution but won't take it. Maybe some coffee will take the edge off." I laughed as I stood to go up to the counter.

"Whoa." Nicole looked up at me. "That comment sounds like it came from some place other than a lack of caffeine. What's going on?"

I sheepishly sat back down in my chair. "Not quite sure. All I know is that I feel angry—at who or what, I have no idea."

"Maybe yourself?" asked Nicole.

"Maybe," I thought out loud. "Maybe I thought you and this process would be a quick-fix to my life. Maybe I thought I'd be farther along by now." I paused. "Maybe I'm mad that I let myself believe that my life *really* can be different."

Nicole looked knowingly at me. "I'm not going to minimize your feelings, but let me reassure you that I've seen this before. It can be a normal phase for many people going through these steps."

"Really?" I said, a little surprised.

"Really," Nicole nodded her head. "I'm asking you to break out of routines that you may have had for years, to radically change your thinking, to reevaluate the way you do things. This can be uncomfortable, and your mind would really like to keep the status quo. It's just rebelling a bit right now, but not to worry—this too shall pass. Give it some time and keep trying to move forward. Pretty soon your mind will start accepting your new reality, and you'll feel much better."

"Promise?" I asked.

"Promise," said Nicole.

"Now I really need coffee." Bev and I stood and walked to

the counter.

When we got back to the table with our steaming mugs Nicole had pulled out a bright purple piece of paper cut out in the shape of a cartoon "talk balloon."

"Remember last week we talked about positive and negative thinking? Well, here's something I keep on my fridge sometimes, just to remind me. It's called How to Have a Positive Attitude."

"I can't believe for a minute that you need help remembering how to be positive," Bev said and leaned over to Nicole.

"It's true," she laughed. "Even I get negative sometimes."

We all gasped.

"So I will share with you my secret on trying to keep my positive attitude intact." She raised the paper up to eye level. "Number one, be where you are. Let go of the past and the future and just enjoy today. Number two, be non-judgmental. Let go of being critical of others. Try to listen and understand. By being less judgmental of others you will be less judgmental of yourself. Number three, own your attitude. Only we control our attitude; it's not genetically or environmentally determined. Every day we choose our attitude about life. Number four, start to eliminate what bothers you. You may be putting up with more things than you realize. Pay attention to what you are tolerating, and take steps towards eliminating it. We talked about that last week, remember?"

We all nodded in agreement.

"Hadn't ever thought about it that way before," Julie said, crinkling her forehead. "Makes sense."

"Number five, listen and trust your inner voice. Learn to shut out other people's voices that you carry in your head. Instead, listen to yourself and take responsibility for what you can and want to do. Number six, really live your values. By living your life according to your values you will develop an attitude of true acceptance of yourself."

"You mean the values we talked about quite a few weeks back?" asked Bev.

"One and the same. Number seven, have fun. Be light. Don't think that's a huge issue around this table."

"Nope, don't think so," we all chuckled.

"Number eight, invest energy in the people you love. This

should have obvious positive results. Number nine, let go—mainly of stuff that really doesn't matter. Don't waste your energy on the unimportant. And lastly, number ten, live in an attitude of love, both for yourself and in turn for others. Consider yourselves all pep-talked." Nicole leaned back in her chair.

"Excellent, I feel better already," Julie sighed.

"It looked like you were talking Julie off the proverbial ledge when we came in." I looked at Nicole.

"Yeah, I guess I'm realizing that big changes may require just that—big changes." Julie sighed.

"It sounds obvious, but Julie is right," Nicole looked at each of us. "In order to reach our goals we'll have to make some sacrifices and compromises, maybe only temporarily, but it can be painful just the same."

"Maybe I need to figure out what my priorities are for the next six months and realize that to have one thing I love, I might have to let go of one thing I like. So by choosing one thing, I wasn't choosing something else. If I wanted to rent a studio I may not have the money for my annual trip to Vegas this year. If I wanted to teach a painting class I may not have the time to go to the gym every day. Maybe that's part of my problem, trying to do and have everything."

"That's life." Nicole shrugged her shoulders.

"Ah, to have nine lives." Julie looked dreamily into her coffee mug.

"Now, going back to your husband's comment about the wife being under foot..." Nicole looked sideways at Bev.

"Nothing gets by you," Bev smiled.

"Nothing. So are you slipping into a new routine yet?" Nicole looked over to me. "I guess this question applies to you, too."

"I think maybe that's the problem," Bev looked a little sheepish. "I think I'm actually missing the routine of my job."

Julie looked confused.

"The first week or so was fine. I was busy catching up on correspondence, I did some spring cleaning, I met lots of friends for coffee, even saw a matinee, but the last couple of days I find myself sort of wandering aimlessly through the house." Bev paused. "I think I'm actually bored. I didn't think it would be like this. It's weird."

"Not at all. Some of us are just wired for routine, and even if we aren't, we've probably had years of structure at work so it's hard to make such a drastic change and not feel a bit weird," Nicole continued. "Maybe for the time being let's not fight your urge to have a little structure. There are plenty of ways to create some routine in your new life. How about a new day-timer to plan your week. Choose one day to be an errand day, one for housework, one or two to work in your yard, one for meeting with friends for coffee or entertaining people in your home, and you can have a day or two that you play it by ear."

"I'll try it, too."

"Good decision, Sam," Nicole agreed. "Now you will obviously have an even more structured schedule since you still have your job, and you have a pretty clear goal that you are going for."

"I'm a little nervous about jumping the gun and filling my days up too quickly, feeling like I'm right back at work," Bev said a bit anxiously. "I should really give this retirement thing an honest try."

"Right. Allow yourself some 'aimless wandering' right now, but I guarantee that there will come a time when you will want to have something meaningful to fill your day. I'm just going to prime the pump and give you some ideas you may want to include into your life."

"Fair enough," Bev agreed.

"You had mentioned travel as being an important goal, so you'll want that on your list, and your family, maybe some further education."

"School?" Bev looked shocked.

"You don't need to go back to university, but you might want to look into your community college. Maybe they have classes on gardening or learning to speak another language, or maybe Sam could teach you how to paint."

"Interesting idea." Bev smiled at me.

"I'm not sure if you could afford me." I smiled back.

Nicole continued. "How about volunteering one day a week or, who knows, you might even look at a second career or a part-time job. Not right away, but maybe down the road somewhere."

Bev grimaced.

"I would recommend that you—well, all of you—should, take time to experiment with all sorts of activities. Don't prejudge whether or not you'll like something. Just try it, and then be mindful of what you enjoyed and why. Start a list of all these activities, and then include them in your weekly or monthly routine."

"So you mean like learning a new skill?" Julie asked.

"It can be," Nicole said, "like rollerblading or baking or making pottery or writing mystery books."

"Oh," Julie nodded.

Nicole pulled a fluorescent-yellow piece of paper out of her binder. "This is what I call my Ten Daily Juicy Habits. It's on my fridge."

"You must have one big fridge to keep all your lists posted!" Julie shook her head.

"Yeah. I have to keep rotating them since I don't have room for everything," Nicole laughed. "So this is something I'm going to have each of you do."

"Juicy habits…?" I asked.

"You could call them just habits, but they're items that you do every day that bring some joy, some *juice*, to your life. Why, you ask, would you want to live juicy every day? Well, as a way of simply taking care of yourself, to ensure that you complete something every day that may be a challenge for you, or to just enjoy the good feeling that it will give you!"

"Let's look at the different areas to give you some ideas for your own list." Nicole looked down at her list. "First, remember your self-care items. So, on your list you'll want some items such as going for a walk or a swim, making a healthy meal, reading a good book, calling a friend who makes you laugh, stuff like that. Second area was to create a bit of a challenge for yourself, maybe something every day that stretches you a little mentally or physically. Also under this area would be doing things that you may not particularly want to do initially, but the outcome is worth it."

"Like working out?" I asked.

"Yes, although that could also fall under the next category of feeling good. On my list I have making my bed. I've never liked doing it and didn't think it was that important to me, but once, on a business trip, I noticed how good I felt when I came back into my hotel room every day and found that my bed was made. So now I take a few minutes and make my bed every morning, and I feel good whenever I go back into my bedroom."

"Try making three beds every morning," Julie sighed.

"Three times the fun!" Nicole carried on. "And then choose something to make yourself feel good. I love spending a few minutes every day petting my cat. He's soft *and* appreciative, so we both get something out of it. Some other examples I have that are under the self-care category are only drinking one cup of coffee a day and getting eight hours of sleep; under challenge I have making my bed and flossing my teeth. I hate that, too," Nicole grimaced. "And under feel good, I have petting my cat and listening to music."

"Daily Juicy Habits—I like that," Bev said matter-of-factly.

"So far, we've touched on the idea that big change requires, well, big change, paying attention to what you enjoy, and including that in your routine,"—Nicole looked at Bev and me—"and our Juicy Habits. Let me top off today with my FQ or Fun Quotient Assessment."

"I like it already," Julie said before enjoying her last sip of coffee.

"I decided that since we had IQ, Intellectual Quotient, and EQ, Emotional Quotient, and even SQ, Spiritual Quotient, we needed an FQ." Nicole pulled yet another list from her binder. "I'll e-mail you my Fun-O-Meter to assess your FQ, but you can start thinking about your idea of fun now."

"I spend lots of time thinking about it. It's actually finding the time to do it—that's the problem." Julie touched her watch.

"Yes, that's a common concern, that and our beliefs around leisure. We think it's a waste of time, too frivolous, with no purpose. We need to see the value in pleasure and joy and not feel guilty. Goes back to the idea that you can't give to people if you are empty. Remember, there can be no other *purpose* for leisure! It is simply for your own pleasure and joy," said Nicole. "Also this adds to our definition of who we are, how to expand our identity, and gives us ideas for a career or ways to spend our retirement. Bev, you especially have lived your life with deadlines, reports, and red tape, and it's time to allow yourself just the pure joy of doing something you love. You've worked hard and you deserve some pleasure. Laughter is especially important. It's very healing, the best medicine, they say."

"Nothing like a good belly laugh; my day isn't complete

without one. Luckily I have Sam to help fill that prescription." Julie poked my arm.

Nicole looked through her paperwork. "Wow, once again we've covered a lot this morning."

"My head has the usual 'full' feeling I get after every meeting," I said, squeezing my temples.

"Next weekend is a long weekend; I assume we're not meeting," Bev said.

Nicole looked around the table. "What's the general consesus?"

"Matt and I are off to his folks', so I won't be around. Jules, isn't your sister coming into town?" I asked.

"Yep, I'm hoping she'll want lots of quality time being Auntie Amy to the kids so that I can get out of the house for a bit."

"Alright, so we'll meet in two weeks and see where everyone is at." Nicole reached back to grab her jean jacket.

"Anyone up for a little fun and leisure?" I opened my wallet. "I think I need a new outfit for my dinner date tonight. On the boyfriend." I pulled out Matt's Visa card and grinned.

WORKBOOK:

TOO MUCH TIME?

Sometimes our biggest enemy is time. During a job search or retirement, we may feel strange not being in our routine. Perhaps creating some structure may help...

If you are looking for some structure in your days, write down ten options to choose from. You may want to go back and look at your "ideal day." Some examples could be coffee and paper in the morning, making follow-up calls, or contacting your network. Write yours below!

1)   6)

2)   7)

3)   8)

4)   9)

5)   10)

Having too many days of 'doing nothing,' filling time watching TV, taking three trips to complete errands instead of one will leave you feeling without purpose. By using these tools and actively deciding your lifestyle choices will provide yourself with what you need to enjoy this time. This will automatically give you purpose. Choose to complete these exercises and do something about them.

Some ideas might include arts and crafts, education, reading, sports, physical activities, travel, adventure...

When Julie eventually graduates she will know that in order to stay on top of her job search it will be important to schedule time for all the activities involved. She will want to set a routine for herself: in the early morning she will make phone calls, then go for a workout, and schedule in-person meetings for the afternoon. This set routine will keep Julie on track and prevent her from procrastinating or doing unnecessary activities. Julie knows that looking for a job is a full-time job in itself.

Bev does not know what type of retirement lifestyle would suit her. She started out just taking things as they came. After several weeks she missed having some idea of what she had planned for the day, saying that sometimes she felt she was wasting time. She decided to create plans for several days out of the week, leaving the rest open, and that balance left her feeling much more excited about her retirement days ahead.

Another way to give yourself a boost is take good care of yourself and fill a n.e.e.d.!

Create your 10 Daily Juicy Habits

Since you'll be doing these activities each day, be sure to add some *juice* to your life!

There are a number of reasons to live juicy every day: 1.to simply take good care of yourself; 2. to ensure you complete something every day that may be a challenge for you; 3. to enjoy the feel-good feeling it will give you. Put at least one thing on your list in each of these categories.

1.   The first area is very important. We are often taught or socialized that taking care of ourselves is very selfish. It's not. Actually, when you don't take care of yourself, you cannot really take care of anyone else. When we are well taken care of we can give more. When you are happiest and have fulfilled your needs, you have more fun caring than you would otherwise.

If you are in retirement or career transition, you can certainly give yourself permission to take care of yourself first. Now that you are not in the nine-to-five routine anymore you have a clean slate to create your day. Write down some self-care items that you can do every day just because you can! Take a nature walk, visit a friend, or read a book. Julie especially needs to do this since she likely forgets about herself after taking care of the kids all day. She and you can start with even ten minutes of quiet time a day.

2.   The second habit that you create could be a challenge but can also make you feel good. It could be exercising, doing the laundry, catching up on errands. This is a chance to get rid of another item on your irritation list. Sam needs to clean out a storage room to make room for her paints.

3.   The third habit is to make yourself feel good. Maybe you have a cat that you can give a good belly rub to every day. They love it, and it can bring you blissful pleasure. Bev enjoys her quiet time in the morning. It makes her feel good and starts the day off right!

Create a list of your Ten Daily Juicy Habits. Remember the categories of self-care, challenge, and feeling good.

1)   6)

2)   7)

3)   8)

4)   9)

5)   10)

Time to assess your FQ (Fun Quotient). Answer 'yes' or 'no' to each of these statements:

I have 'fun' things in every room of my house.

I have at least one fun CD/tape to listen to while driving.

I know ten fun things I like to do, and make it a habit to laugh, or have fun daily.

I have fun 'connecting' with my friends or new people.

I know ten fun environments I enjoy being in.

I have at least one fun outfit to wear.

Going after my dream is fun for me!

I have time for play every day.

The people in my life encourage my play and fun activities.

My work environment stimulates my sense of fun.

I have a favorite fun thing/place in my house.

When I wake up I see something that is fun and makes me chuckle.

I know at least one person who I am guaranteed to laugh with.

I love to make another person's day fun for them.

I have an attitude of play. I take my work seriously, myself lightly.

I only watch movies/TV that uplift, teach, or make me laugh.

I know how to change my attitude to fun/play/positive.

I have a closet full of fun things to do.

When I'm in a serious situation, I smile on the inside.

I love to laugh till my face hurts!

What did you score? If you answered 'no' to more than ten, turn up your "fun-o-meter." How? By trying new things. Open your mind and life to new adventure. Ask someone who enjoys life how they make it so. Do one thing today that increases joy in your life.

Some things that may add fun to your life are "I Love Lucy" reruns, lick & stick tattoos, musical theatre, making milkshakes, singing!

Also visit www.sherriolsen.com for a guaranteed laugh!

CHAPTER SEVEN

The long weekend was just what the doctor ordered. I needed a change of scenery and some downtime as I continued to wrestle with all of the choices I had rattling around in my head. The one thing I wasn't prepared for was the blank look on Matt's parents' faces when I tried to explain why I had gone to part-time and was even contemplating leaving a "perfectly good job" to be a painter. I hadn't realized how difficult it was going to be convincing people that being a painter was a valid career, a job, actual work. I guess on some level I understood since even I had some problems believing that you could make a living doing what you loved. It seemed too easy. Some days, I almost felt guilty. By the end of the weekend, I think I had calmed his folks down and they seemed satisfied with my response that I was going to give the whole artist thing a try, and that if it didn't work I could always go find another "real job."

I was looking forward to meeting with the girls this morning as I hadn't heard from Bev and had barely touched base with Julie since our last meeting.

"Good morning!" Bev and Nicole were already here.

"Good morning, sunshine." Bev smiled.

"Don't you look chipper this morning." Nicole moved her bag so I could sit down.

"Thank you."

"Good week?" Nicole asked.

"Yeah, I made some contacts with three galleries that are all interested in showing my work. They're small, but, still, who knows what will come out of it?"

"For sure. That's great, Sam," said Nicole.

Just then the door jingled open and Julie burst in. Her hair was tied back, and she was trying to juggle her car keys, binder, and cell phone and was a little out of breath.

"Sorry, girls, am I late?"

"I just got here." I took the binder from her hand and laid it on the table. "Why do you always look like you just got back from 'saving the world' or are on the run from the Men in Black?"

"Are you mocking me?" She peered over her sunglasses at me.

"Maybe."

"I have a perfectly good reason why I look like this today. You're going to be sorry that you made fun of me." She punched my arm. "I had to stop by the university," she paused for effect, "to hand-deliver my registration application!"

We all let out a holler, much to the surprise of everyone else in the coffee shop.

"Oh, my gosh, you're serious?" I asked.

"Totally. They have my check, and there's no turning back."

"Way to go, Julie." Nicole looked genuinely pleased.

"So, I don't want to be the pessimist, but how are you going to do this?" asked Bev.

"Well, we're selling the house."

"What!" I said almost too quickly.

"Mark and I have been talking about it ever since the divorce, and now just seems like a perfect time."

"And you'll be living...?" I questioned.

"With my sister."

"Amy?" I said, not believing that she would move out of the city.

"No, the other one," she said, leaning in to calm me down. "Debbie and Brent have that mother-in-law suite in the basement and it'll be empty at the end of next month. They've offered to let us stay there for as long as we need and basically only help out with the utilities."

"That'll be cozy," I grimaced.

"I know, but it's the only way that I can afford to go back to school full-time," she said and looked at Nicole. "The sacrifice will be worth the reward, right?"

"Absolutely."

"And, I will probably have to get some cheesy, little job to help out. I had to borrow the tuition from my parents, and I'd like to pay them off as soon as possible."

"You must be so excited," said Nicole.

"I am. It's a big change … hopefully for a big change!"

"This is truly good news." Nicole crossed her arms. "Now all of you have made some sort of step towards your goal. You're on your way."

"It's still a process, though," Bev said quietly.

"Yes, and by that statement, I take it that you are still struggling with a few things? Still settling into your new life?"

"The things we talked about last time were great. I've thought some more about how to have structure in my day," she said and paused, "but now, just lately, I'm actually feeling a bit lonely. I miss the daily contact I had with people at work."

"Understandable. You're a very social person." Nicole looked around the table. "You all are. So when you lose or transition away from one group of people you need to think of ways to create new communities within your life."

"No man is an island."

"Exactly, Julie. Just like we've been thinking of activities to fill our lives, we need to think of people to fill our lives. You can look into your local community association for ideas of ways to meet new people. Why not start a book club or find a hiking group or maybe volunteer to sit on the board of your favorite arts foundation. One of my favorites is to volunteer your skills. Like helping kids to read or holding babies at the hospital. The bottom line is to be open to meeting new people, and I guarantee new people will appear."

"If you're really desperate you could actually call *me* sometime for lunch," I feigned hurt.

"I never want to call for fear that I may be interrupting your creative flow," said Bev.

"Whatever. Food is never an interruption." I smiled.

"Speaking of which," Julie said, looking around at each of us, "do you realize that we don't have coffee yet?"

"Good grief, we must rectify that immediately." I stood up.

"Can you get me a dark roast, black." Bev pushed some change over to me.

"No problem."

Julie looked over at Nicole. "Anything for you?"

"I couldn't wait for my java this morning and already had one at home, so just an apple juice, please."

"Coming right up."

When we converged back on the table with beverages in hand, Nicole started. "I am just so proud of all of you. This may be the hardest part, the first step."

"I hope so." I sipped slowly from my steaming cup.

"But I will encourage you to keep clarifying your destination and keeping this vision in sight." She popped the lid off her juice. "If you haven't already, write it down. This alone puts you into the top three per cent of the population. Then put a date or a deadline that you want to achieve this, and, again, be very specific. Then stop and think about what obstacles you may need to overcome. You may decide that you need additional skills, like Julie, or more knowledge in a particular area and support from others."

"Like my good sister, who is taking in her poor student sibling?" said Julie.

"Yes, that's a very tangible support that you needed. We all need to get better at asking for things we need." She sipped from her bottle of juice. "Next, we should plan out action steps, and finally we should start taking them. It's that simple."

"It always sounds simple when we're sitting around this table, but when Monday morning rolls around sometimes it's hard not to fall right back into your old routines." I added another packet of sugar to my coffee. "I think I'm just lazy."

"I doubt it."

"So do I, Julie." Nicole looked at me. "I would say that complacency is a better word."

"'Complacency.' Doesn't sound as bad as 'lazy.' I'll take it." I smiled and slapped my hand down on the table.

"It's easy enough for all of us to become complacent. Maybe you don't want to be different than anyone else, you want to go along with the crowd, blend in." Nicole paused. "This is something you learned, and it has no value. Take control, and choose to be and feel what you want. The opposite of complacency is confidence and self-value. It's like the story of the farmer's dog yelping in pain as he lies on the front porch. A neighbor walks up to the farmer to ask why he doesn't help his dog, who is obviously in pain. The farmer responded, 'I've tried. I've picked him up and moved him, but he just keeps going back to sit on that nail.'"

"This is why I'm a cat person," I joked.

"People who sit and complain about their lives are just sitting on their nails, not wanting to change them. If you are doing something that is hurting you, stop doing it. Choose something else. It's so simple and yet so profound."

"Right." We all agreed.

"Start to be aware of the percentage of positive thoughts versus negative thoughts that you have on a daily basis. If you have a negative thought, quickly substitute it for a positive one. How, you ask?" Nicole paused like leading up to a punchline. "Use your mind! Choose a better thought. This becomes a habit once we have done it for a while." Nicole jotted this down for our homework. "By doing this we take control of our emotions and our actions. It all starts in your head. Did you know that we can think thousands of times faster than we can talk?" asked Nicole.

"You'd hardly believe it with the things that come out of my mouth!" said Julie sarcastically.

"Well, I'm glad to hear we're not lazy," Bev said. "Still, I feel a bit aimless at times. I know I'm retired, but I still need to feel like I have a purpose."

"Maybe now more than ever." Nicole started writing again, then looked up. "How about creating your own personal mission statement?"

"What? That sounds a bit 'corporate,' don't you think?" I asked.

"Don't panic. Having your own mission statement is just chunking together your values. You still have those written down, right?" Nicole looked at each of us, and we all nodded. "Good. So take your values and add a verb. This can articulate your purpose in retirement or simply give you direction and focus in life."

"Do I need to put this on my business cards?" asked Julie.

"Not unless you want to. No one ever needs to see it except you. As an example," Nicole said looking at Bev, "you can define your retirement lifestyle by putting your values together. Start with: *The purpose of my life is to honor my values of...*, choose your top four, by…, say how you express those values, *so that*…, this could be for a group of people, a cause, or just for yourself." Nicole could see that we still looked a little confused and added, "An example would be, *'The purpose of my life is to honor my values of being adept, connected, feeling good and creating an impact by volunteering, spending my time with family and friends as well as traveling.'*"

"I never imagined that retirement was going to be so complicated." Bev leaned back in her chair. "Gord and I spent so much time working out the financial end of things—Could we still contribute to our retirement plans? Would we have to dip into our savings? What about my pension? Could we still afford the cabin? No one warned me about the emotional and spiritual side of retirement, that I'd have to change more than my spending habits."

Nicole nodded. "Just think about how much time and energy we invest into our careers. Starting back in high school, we went to career counselors, took workshops, and attended seminars. We went to university or college or a trade school for years. Then we trained on the job, and most of us experienced ongoing learning to adapt to our changing environments and to keep ourselves marketable. Then when it comes time for retirement we give about as much thought to it as we do to choosing chicken or fish for the farewell party. It's crazy. Most people are woefully unprepared for one of life's biggest transitions. We just expect to slip comfortably into a totally different reality."

"So true," Bev agreed, "especially if you don't have control over when it happens."

"That certainly adds another dimension, but now you all are leaps and bounds ahead," Nicole said, smiling. "You have the tools to make any transition that much more smoothly and, quite frankly, just to live a better life."

"So if we have all the tools we need for success, why are we all still scared?" I asked. I felt like I had all the head knowledge, but it still wasn't totally translating into action. Everything we had talked about made sense and could actually work. I think I knew that on some level but still felt frozen in indecision.

"We've taken steps, made progress," added Julie.

"I agree, but I think we're all still holding back in some area or areas of our lives. It's like we're not one hundred per cent convinced that we can do this or even that we deserve this," I said.

"This?" questioned Bev.

"This ... dream-life, this utopia," I said.

"It's natural to feel uncertain at times. What can you do to ease your fears? What is it asking you to pay attention to? To prepare for? What action step can you take to ease this?" Nicole smiled. "Sam's right; you've all made significant progress." Nicole pulled out her datebook. "We only have one more meeting—boy, time flies—so why don't you all think about some areas or issues that we haven't covered or things you'd like us to revisit and e-mail them to me in the next couple of days. We'll touch on those topics as well as do a summary of what we've talked about."

It was hard to believe that we had been meeting for a few months already, and as I looked at both of my friends I realized how significantly we had all changed. I felt good about how far I'd come, but I still felt like I had a few loose ends that needed to be tied up. I guess everyone felt the same way, as the topics that they wanted Nicole to cover were already flying around the table.

WORKBOOK:

YOU'VE GOT A FRIEND...

Surround yourself with a blanket of friends. Let them support you through this transition. Identify who in your life positively influences you. Now, call them! If you want to build your community of friends, ask yourself, "Would someone want me to be their friend?" How can you have more meaningful relationships?

You can design your community by asking yourself, what type of community am I seeking? Is it around activities, beliefs, a social cause? What do you want to achieve through your community? What qualities and characteristics of individuals within this community are you looking for? Is yours a coffee club, like Julie, Sam, and Bev, or is it volunteering, or maybe a team sport?

Project a few years from now. Write down five characteristics, qualities, skills, or achievements that you gained because you took part in a specific community, group, or activity. Be specific. What do you want to see for yourself in five years?

ARE YOU REACHING FOR THE STARS OR JUST TURNING ON A NITE LIGHT?

Sometimes when we are setting goals we sway to one of two extremes. Often we set goals that are too far away for us, which leaves us feeling that it is not worth it to even try or that it is too great a stretch for our minds to imagine. The other extreme is to make the goal so minimal that it becomes *de*motivating. Keep your goals at eye level, and break it into the individual steps required to reach it. If your goal is finding a new job, write a résumé, conduct research, write down your network, make phone calls, apply for positions, follow up. Is your goal at eye level? Break it into specific and attainable steps.

For retirement, once you've identified your successful retirement, what steps do you need to take to achieve that? Bev needs to try new activities and to figure out how to co-exist with her husband full time in the house. Maybe they agree to each leaving the house to allow the other personal quiet time.

Think about some areas where you are 'sitting on a nail, yelping.' Is it your job, your weight, your relationships, your happiness. Write them down. What can you choose to do to 'get off the nail'? List the first three steps here and put a date beside it as a commitment to get it done.

Choose to eliminate complacency. Most of us want a worry-free retirement or a new job. What is the reason for you to do this? Because it brings you pleasure! Because you choose and decide it to be so! When we aim for pleasure, we put a stop to doing things out of perceived duty and obligation that would give rise to resistance and rebelliousness. Do you want to dislike your job or your life? Then choose to define what you want and then take steps towards it. You *can* do this!

WILL A PURPOSE STATEMENT HELP?

What is your reason to get up in the morning? To feel good? Make a difference? Make money? Learn something new? Be immersed in your favorite activity, or task?

So many reach for a goal, always wondering what it is but not sure how to obtain it. The meaning of life or work begins with these exercises. If I had a dollar for every time I heard someone say that they wanted to make a difference but didn't know what that meant, I'd be rich! To answer this, it begins with knowing yourself, by completing the exercises in this book. Create your purpose statement: draw your favorite espresso beverage—each layer is a verb, the cup is your value, and whom your purpose is for is whom you are serving the beverage to!

Now you have your purpose statement, the last piece is to ask yourself, who would you like to serve it to?

For example, my favorite latté has a layer of espresso, whole milk, and steamed milk. Each layer is a verb that describe something that excites me, something full of meaning and purpose. Learning, service, and connection describe Julie. It goes in your favorite mug, which denotes something you value, something you stand for. Go back and look at your values list. Growth could be an example of a value. Who you serve it to could be the group of people you would like to contribute to, or even the industry you want to work in. Perhaps it is the oil and gas industry or to volunteer for a not-for-profit group. The purpose statement would read: I get up in the morning to learn, serve, and connect with others in order to grow and to contribute to the not-for-profit sector.

What are you afraid of? List them *all* here. It could be money, losing friends, having to move, not being good enough, skilled enough, smart enough, etc. Now, go back to chapter three and complete the +10 to -10 exercise. Now have a real look at what you are afraid of and see if you can plan for it, to avoid it or deal with it.

What are your reasons for making any life change you are considering? The longer the list, the more naturally motivated you will be.

CHAPTER EIGHT

I was trying not to let the gray sky and cold drizzle of rain dampen my spirit as I drove towards the café this last morning of meeting with our wise life coach. The sound of my windshield wipers lulled me into reminiscing about what had happened in my life in just a few short months. I hadn't realized just how complacent I had become with myself, not really making decisions, at least not hard ones. I knew in my heart that I wasn't happy. I was frozen by fear and must have had that proverbial deer-in-the-headlights look on my face for the last ten years as my life had just come at me. I was seeing more clearly now as I rounded the corner looking for a parking spot. I was overwhelmed with feelings of disappointment that the last ten years of my life were so far removed from where I was heading now. If I was honest, though, I still had moments and days where the fear still pulled at me, and my 'inner critic' almost convinced me that I should give it up and go back to my safe reality. As I turned the key in the ignition and reached for my purse I hoped that Nicole would have some final words of wisdom that would carry me through my anxiety. I felt in that moment how important it was, these choices I was making and these changes I was setting in motion. I was altering my tomorrow today and starting to live the life I was always meant to live. Nothing was more important. I pushed my car door closed and walked quickly towards the warmth of the café. "Good morning, everyone."

"How's that seasonal affect disorder? Weather bringing you down this morning?" Julie said shaking off her umbrella. "Sam gets grumpy when the sun doesn't shine," she explained to Bev and Nicole.

"I'm fine. You know my answer for whatever ails ya?"

"Coffee!" they all said in unison.

"Ah, you know me too well." I pulled off my damp, fleece

jacket and headed towards the counter.

Julie followed. "So this is it. The last 'meeting of the minds,' so speak. How do you feel?"

"Generally pretty good. I'm pointed in the right direction but still have these urges to slip back into my old, safe life every once and a while. You?"

"I feel a bit like the slow kid in the class since I'm just starting to make some changes." Julie dug some money out of her pocket. "I agree with everything Nicole has said, but putting it all into practice seems like a lot of work sometimes."

"It does and it is, but what are our options? Keep doing what we're doing and getting what we've got?"

"Hmmm…" Julie savored the idea and a sip of her coffee.

"The bottom line is that we all want to take the path of least resistance. The easy road." I slipped the change over to Julie.

"I have to believe this will get easier, though." Julie led the way back to our table. "I mean, once this 'new life' becomes our reality it won't seem like so much work."

We carefully sat our full coffee cups down on the table, and Nicole looked up.

"We were just talking about how this still feels like work some days. Changing our thinking, shifting our beliefs, positive affirmations, daily habits, taking risks … it's going to get easier, right?" asked Julie.

"That's really up to you and how you look at things," Nicole reassured us.

"Fair enough." Bev smiled. "So what final pearls of wisdom are you going to bestow on us?"

"Well, like I said last week, you have good tools that enabled you to all make your first step and will keep you moving forward, but now we'll learn to overcome any blips on the screen that come our way. It's our mind and perspective on things that can get in our way." Nicole paused. "Your mind, your thoughts, beliefs, mental habits—everything starts there."

"I know I made the right decision to go back to school, but every day a voice in my head will whisper something to me like, 'You're too old this, you'll never graduate, and what makes you think you deserve a better life anyway?'" Julie looked into her mug. "It's hard to shut that off. And what's worse is when I see both of you making such great changes and I feel sort of left behind."

"What are you talking about? You know that regardless of how I look on the outside, I'm usually a wreck on the inside," I added quickly.

"Not to mention that you have all these other changes going on in your life right now, albeit not all positive ones," Bev piped in.

"Everyone moves at different speeds and you have to remember that even though I had been toying with the idea for months, I still had a hard time transitioning. You didn't really see all the months of struggle I had, only a few long weeks of panic and anger and then the end result of my layoff, which sort of forced me into making a decision."

"Exactly," Nicole agreed. "I know it's hard. You need to not compare your journey to other people's. Focus on you and your accomplishments instead."

Good words. I knew how easy it was to look at everyone around me and judge *my* progress by *their* lives! I needed to remember that every journey is unique and that there is no one timeline. I had to stop wasting my energies on comparison and competition. This was especially difficult some days with Julie and Bev.

As if she was reading my mind Nicole continued, "You are in a unique situation where you are all stepping out onto your new paths around the same time, so comparisons will be tempting. You can be an amazing support to each other if you don't let competition or jealousy get in the way."

"There's enough success to go around for everyone!"

"Right on, Sam, and I can attest to the fact that there is nothing more fulfilling than living a successful life and then helping others to live theirs. Remember the 'no man is an island' philosophy."

"I prefer to think of myself as more of a peninsula," I said, smiling. "At first glance I may appear to be an island, but I still have one finger connected to the mainland."

"Oh, brother." Julie rolled her eyes.

"I know we've already touched on fear, but maybe we need to go a little deeper with that." Nicole flipped back through her notes. "I think we talked briefly about fear when we first started meeting, but it sounds like it's lurking around in your lives again. First you need to realize that fear manifests itself in lots of different ways, rarely as what we think of as fear. It appears as anxiety, sadness, depression, and, most commonly, anger. So when you start to feel any of those emotions stop and ask yourself what you may be afraid of."

Anger is really fear. When I thought about it, that made a lot of sense, not only in my trying to make this transition but also in all areas of my life. When I got angry at Matt, if I was really honest with myself, nine times out of ten, it was based in my insecurity that he may leave.

"So, if I'm feeling depressed about my life, I'm really afraid of …," Julie's voice trailed off, "success?"

"Which is more powerful than fear of failure," said Nicole.

We all looked a little confused so she continued. "Let's play fill in the blank. If I succeed…," she started and glanced around the table at our blank stares. "We all have these beliefs about success, many of which come from our past, our parents, and our peer group. Most are no longer true, but if we cling to them we have an excuse to stay where we are. Some people believe that if they become successful everyone would be jealous of them and hate them or that their family wouldn't understand them or that they would have to move away or they might lose the people they care about."

"That's an interesting idea," said Bev.

"There is a fine line between fear of failure and fear of success. Underneath both of these fears is the feeling that we don't deserve success, that we don't deserve happiness, a career, or love," said Nicole.

Fear of success. Looking around the table I could tell that we were all thinking about that one. The status quo is so much simpler. People already had us in a box—mother, student, banker, teacher. It can be frustrating trying to change people's view of us. It can be equally hard trying to change our own views of ourselves.

"And this moves right into our self-esteem. How would you define self-esteem?"

"How we see ourselves," said Bev.

"How other people see us," I added.

"Or our perceptions of how other people see us. Good. And what does that all encompass?" Nicole probed.

"Physical, mental, spiritual," Julie said confidently.

"Right. This breaks down even further into all the details of our lives—what we wear, where we work, what kind of car we drive, what we eat, the kind of people we invite into our lives, how we talk to ourselves, how we let other people treat us." Nicole let that sink in. "It all goes back to our self-image. Where do you think we get our self-image from?"

"Same place as where we get our views on success—past, parents, and peer group," said Bev.

"Exactly." Nicole took a quick sip of her coffee. "Add to that list—our environment and all things media, fashion magazines, music videos, and movie stars. All contribute to this rather warped idea of what it means to be beautiful or successful or happy."

"How do we fight it? This is the world we live in." I leaned back on my chair.

"We have to start telling ourselves the truth," Julie said with conviction.

"First we have to figure out what the truth is," I said.

"Yes, so let's stop and talk about what our lives would look like if we had good self-esteem." Nicole looked at each of us.

"I'd have more confidence," said Julie.

"I suppose I'd be content with how I looked," I added.

"Accepting of my strengths *and* weakness," Bev continued.

"The ability to truly celebrate other people's success speaks volumes for your own self-esteem." Julie looked up sheepishly. "I'm working on that."

"Figuring out what you're good at and being true to that." I reached for my cup.

After a short pause Nicole started, "Keep building on this definition of self-esteem. A good exercise is to write down all the aspects, qualities, or characteristics you would be to have self-esteem or personal well-being."

Nicole went on to encourage us to start implementing all of our homework into our lives and we would start to see a huge difference, like watering the seeds of healthy self-esteem. This would give us a fresh perspective on ourselves, and we'd start to see how much we've grown. We had to stop being so hard on ourselves and remove the unrealistic measuring sticks in our lives to focus on the real picture of who we were. She said that this would be something that would be good to keep each other accountable for, to make sure we all had an accurate picture of ourselves.

"I can't emphasize this enough. If you have a poor self-esteem it is difficult to really succeed. Primarily because you won't believe that you are worthy of it, and that will lead to years of self-sabotage and displaced anger," said Nicole.

"Which is really fear," I said matter-of-factly.

"You were listening." Nicole poked my arm. "Without healthy self-esteem you won't properly develop your gifts or a sense of personal well-being. You'll struggle with your work, your play, your relationships, your life. If you don't see yourself accurately you certainly don't see other people accurately. This will lead to misunderstanding and mistrust."

"How do we change the picture in our head?" asked Bev.

"Start with your self-talk, what's rolling around in your head. Affirmations are a great way to overcome some of our distorted beliefs, but it can be a little embarrassing at first." Nicole crinkled her forehead.

"It's always easier to put yourself down rather than build yourself up. Am I right?" Julie looked around the table.

"Right on," Nicole concurred. "So just start with one affirmation and write it down ten times, and then say it in your head throughout the day, and hopefully you'll get to the point where you can even say it out loud. It sounds extreme, but we are literally having to reprogram your brain, and, like creating any new habit, repetition is the key. It takes twenty-one days to form a habit, so make it fun by making it into a jingle and singing it in the shower."

"I don't think my new label includes singer." Julie scrunched her forehead.

"You're a runner, right? So think of it more as training for a marathon, which brings up another interesting topic that we really haven't touched on." Nicole glanced at her watch. "Does anyone have other commitments, or can we linger a bit this morning?"

We all nodded in the affirmative and she carried on. "We've talked a lot about mental health, but haven't really explored the physical or spiritual side of our lives and living a life of balance."

"Am I gonna need more coffee for this?" I asked, already standing up.

"I think we should all get a refill and meet back here for the second half," Bev grabbed her empty cup.

"We're going to squeeze every last thing out of you that we can," Julie laughed and looked at Nicole. "At least let me buy your last cup of java with us."

"Sure, balance schmalance, what's one more cup of coffee in the big scheme of things," I said.

We all raised our empty mugs to that one.

WORKBOOK:

1. If you have begun your transition, what are some of the "blips" that are appearing on your screen? *I'm too busy. I don't have the money. I'm not educated enough.* Look at each one and decide if there is something that you can do to eliminate it.

2. Are there people in your life that are also going through a transition and need a cheerleader? List the people and ways you can support them. Nothing is more fulfilling than living a fulfilled life and helping others to live theirs.

3. Write down all the aspects, qualities, and characteristics you would need to have self-esteem and personal well-being. Be specific and clear. Remember, image precedes reality!

4. Find ways to give a dose of self-esteem to yourself each day. It can be as simple as mentally or verbally acknowledging yourself. I love curling up in my down quilt every night when I go to bed and imagining it as a warm blanket of love surrounding me!

5. Write down three to five affirmations in the present tense, as if they already were true. For example, *I am a successful artist. I am an excellent student with an A average.*

Is your inner critic hassling you? I love to play Wac-a-mole with it. Do you remember that game in the fair grounds? You have a big club, and as the mole pops up, you WHACK them! The faster you WHACK, the more points you make. If you are going to be grumpy or have an inner critic or feel negative, you may as well make a game out of getting over it. As you do this in your head, you'll likely end up chuckling to yourself, which will automatically change your state. And when you get a chance, go play this very physical game next time the carnival is in town. You'll work up a sweat.

CHAPTER NINE

With our mugs brimming with fresh, hot coffee we all settled back into our chairs for part two of our conversation.

"Before we jump into the idea of creating balance in our lives by integrating the physical, mental, and emotional, another thing I'm going to encourage you all to do is to look into personality assessment." Nicole pulled a questionnaire out of her binder. "We don't have time to do it now, but there are lots of good books and Web sites that look at the various personality types."

"Don't you think that's a bit like a horoscope?" I asked. "I just don't think you can squeeze the entire population into four neat categories. Doesn't leave a lot of room for individuality."

"I disagree," Bev interjected. "At work last year we had to do a personality test during this workshop we were taking, and I was surprised at just how accurate it was. It nailed me, and I was a doubter, too."

"I don't think any test should put you in a box and say this is who you are, you'll never change and you're just like twenty-five per cent of the population," Nicole continued. "All they do is open your eyes to not only your 'type' but other people's 'types' and help you to see that it's useful to work within your strengths and to acknowledge your weaknesses. There are lots of books that will take your type and give you ideas for career paths. I've done them regularly throughout my life and have seen very little deviation. You may go through experiences that cause you to have some flexibility and adaptability from, say, extraverted to introverted, for a period of time, but if who you are, at the core, is extraverted, the assessment will indicate that, and it's best to use it to your advantage."

"Everyone in my department had to do it, and it was interesting to look at other people's personality types and realize that one wasn't better than the next, only different." Bev looked at me. "It helped me to communicate better with some of my colleagues and definitely my boss. When I looked at how each of them naturally communicated and handled conflict, I could better adapt, and I got more positive results." Bev saw my skepticism. "We are all unique within our 'type,' but there are just some things that come more naturally to us—the way we make friends, the way we like our life organized, the way we show emotion."

"It can actually be quite freeing to see yourself under a label," Nicole quickly kept going. "I know it sounds like an oxymoron to be free within a 'box,' but once you realize that everyone is made up differently—being outgoing versus more shy, being a thinker versus a feeler, or being a leader versus a follower—and if you can be sensitive to these different qualities in other people, it can make your life a whole lot easier. This is simply another tool to help you understand yourself better and, as a bonus, will help you in understanding other people, as well."

"Hmmm..." I was becoming convinced.

"I think as a culture we put a lot of focus on trying to change people, to get people to work on their weaknesses. Instead, why not continually improve and develop our innate skills and strengths that we most enjoy and become a master at it. This can increase our happiness factor." Nicole paused. "Why not pour our time and energy into what we already do well and improve that and worry less about what other people do better than ourselves. If everyone did that, the world would be full of people who were genuinely good at and happy in their jobs."

"Makes sense, I guess," I agreed.

"I'll send you some suggestions as to where you can find a good personality assessment." Nicole took a sip of her coffee. "So, going back to the idea of balance and integration in our lives..."

"You're not going to tell us to take up yoga and start eating tofu, are you?" Julie looked over the rim of her coffee mug.

"Maybe..." Nicole smirked. "Anytime we start making significant changes you can count on it affecting our body, mind, and spirit. We've talked a lot about changing our thought patterns. We also need to consider changing how we treat our bodies and spirit, too."

"I have to admit," Julie leaned in, "when I'm unhappy I get so restless, I can't sleep, I lose my appetite, and generally feel lethargic. Ever since I've made this decision to go back to school I've been absolutely exhausted."

Bev added, "I thought that being at home more, I'd eat better, exercise, and basically take better care of myself, but it hasn't happened that way. I find it's a real discipline to just get off the sofa some days."

"When your mind is overwhelmed with stress it is going to trickle down into your body," said Nicole, "and your spirit. I don't think we can compartmentalize our lives and say my eating won't affect my productivity at work, or my lack of attention to my soul won't affect my body. It all runs together."

"What are your recommendations, Dr. Nicole?" Julie asked.

"First, listening to yourself. Pay attention to when you are tired or hungry or full. Most people are out of touch with their bodies and souls. We are too busy to actually hear what they are saying to us every day."

"My body is mostly saying 'feed me,'" I said, laughing, "but maybe I'm misinterpreting."

"Your body probably *is* saying 'feed me.'" Nicole leaned over and pointed at what was left of my sourdough bagel with extra cream cheese. "The problem is what you're feeding it. I'm not big on any particular diet or exercise routine, but I do think that there is nothing that will affect your life more positively or negatively than how you treat your body."

"It's the container for you mind," added Bev.

"Exactly," Nicole agreed enthusiastically, "so treat it accordingly. It's got to be an entirely different way of doing things, not a three-month diet regime." She smiled at me. "You may want to look into yoga—excellent for stretching both the mind and body—or swimming or just a brisk walk every day. And when it comes to eating, everything in moderation."

"Moderation is a relative term." I smiled.

"Do I need to spell out a daily diet for you?" Nicole scolded me and then smiled. "Again, lot's of good books you can look at, but the bottom line is to just be aware of what you are putting in your body and how much."

"How does the spiritual side work into all of this?" asked Julie.

"A hugely overlooked area in our lives, I feel," Bev interjected.

"Perhaps," said Nicole, "although I think that's changing. People are beginning to realize that attention to our soul or spirit is integral to our quality of life. Let me just say that spirituality is a very personal thing. I would encourage you to explore it further in your own life, if you haven't already. Spend time every day in silence or meditation or doing something creative. Live a life of gratitude, give generously of your time, talent, and treasure, get outside, and enjoy nature. When something's 'off' in one area of my life I know I have to look at all the areas and make some adjustments. When it comes to our mind, body, and soul everything affects everything."

I had to admit that I felt most at peace, most alive, most connected when I was doing what I loved—creating. Many of my most spiritual moments occurred when I was alone with my canvas, my colors, and my thoughts. I could paint for hours, and instead of feeling drained, I was renewed. Part of my problem was pouring myself into one part of my life and completely forgetting the rest.

"So it's all about balance and spending time concentrating on all the areas," I added.

"Hard to do when you have other people demanding your attention," said Julie. "When you have kids pulling on your sleeve every minute of the day, it's hard to take time for yourself."

"It all comes back to your choices and how to manage your time," said Nicole. "You need to decide if you are worth it, if you deserve it—deserve to be healthy, to be happy. We need to remember that we cannot give what we do not have. You're no good to anyone if you're tired or sick or empty."

"What we give to other people should come from an overflow of what we already have. You can't give anyone else fuel if you have an empty tank." Bev sipped from her coffee mug.

"Good analogy," said Nicole. "Can I use it?"

"If you give me the credit!"

"Done." Nicole closed her binder. "What else do we need to touch on?"

We all thought for a moment.

Suddenly Nicole added, "We've talked about creativity, which can free us from our fears and explore what could be undiscovered territory for us."

"Got that covered," I said. "When I look at kids, they are all hugely creative and have no inhibitions. They draw on their bedroom walls, they dance to whatever is on the radio, they sing while driving in the car. As they get older, we beat it out of them with criticism and boundaries and rules."

"This is so true, Sam. For me creation is a form of meditation." Nicole paused. "When I paint—and I'm definitely not a painter—I forget about the grumpy client I had earlier that day or that I should lose five more pounds or whatever. It's just me and my art. Very freeing."

"Hmm… We can't all be as talented and creative as Sam." Bev sounded frustrated.

"There are hundreds of ways to be creative. Try a new recipe, paint your bedroom, plant a flower garden, doodle when you're on the phone. You're not being graded on it or trying to sell it. Writing is another way to create, and, again, you don't have to sell a screenplay. You just have to write … anything, something." Nicole looked around the table. "I really encourage you to keep journaling. Getting your thoughts down on paper can sometimes simplify things, bring you clarity, maybe a solution to a problem you couldn't find when it was just rattling around in your head."

"I've tried doing free-association writing before and it's amazing what comes out," said Julie with surprise.

"It's a great exercise to just put pen to paper and purge, so to speak." Nicole fiddled with her pen. "When you get all the clutter out of your head you have room for the 'good stuff.' The world we live in inundates us with so many images and words. It's healthy to get them out every once in a while to make room for the important rather than what we perceive as urgent."

"So much to remember." I tapped my forehead.

"I know it seems a bit overwhelming now, but soon this will just be a way of life for you," Nicole reassured me.

"You're insight has truly been invaluable," added Bev. "It's made this transition so much smoother."

"It's been my pleasure working with all of you, and I look

forward to seeing where your lives lead you." Nicole pulled out her datebook. "I'd really like to schedule a meeting with you all again in a few months to congratulate you all on your success."

"An optimist to the end." I shook my head.

"I'm nothing if not consistent," Nicole said as she smiled and flipped through her book.

As we all pulled out our calendars I was a bit sad to see this end but excited to realize that if I'd come this far in a few short months, what lay ahead was more promising that I'd first thought. It *was* possible to change your life by changing your thinking. To dream and then make that dream your reality. I had a new set of glasses on, and the future looked bright.

WORKBOOK:

Fireworks of Life

Have you ever been to a fireworks display? Isn't it wondrous when the sky lights up full of brilliant colors and designs. Each one of us has an opportunity to create bright sparkling lives that can shine brilliantly and give us a feeling of happiness by living our lives the way we want.

Is your firework of life bursting with color and splendor? Or does it fizzle out? Sometimes it can be difficult to balance all areas of our lives. What words do you use when you think of maintaining all areas of your life? Choice. Responsibility. Feeling good. Want. Should. We all decide consciously, or not, how we choose to spend out time juggling work, self, family, health, and goals. Are these areas something you want to maintain, or think you should? Are you saying to yourself, "I want to feel good, find a good job, be healthy, but it's so hard to fit everything in?" Read on as this illustrates one way to manage all areas of our lives.

Consider the basic components of a firework: There is a cylinder or ball called a shell that houses the inner workings of the firework. It is filled with individual stars, which are surrounded by an explosive mechanism, with a fuse in the middle to ignite it all. Consider that each star is an area of your life: "peace of mind," "health and energy," "loving relationships," "financial freedom," "worthy goal and ideals," "self-knowledge," and "career." Add any others that are important to you. Now, define each of these areas of your life. What does health and energy mean to you? Is it exercising twice a week? Eating a salad at lunch? What about worthy goals? Define each area of your life, according to your standards.

If you were to rate each star according to your definition between 1 and 10, with 10 being absolutely no need for improvement, what would your score be?

Would your firework of life explode beautifully and freely in the atmosphere? Or would it fizzle out before it left the ground?

Maybe some days are better than others are. If you could improve one area of your life, how much difference would it make? Each star is intertwined and dependent on the stars surrounding them. If you do not take the time to take care of your health, or leave work on time, etc., how will that effect your family life? Your job? Your quality of life? Could you be happier and healthier with a zest for life? Would you gain satisfaction by balancing the areas of your life that are important to you? By being responsible for your choices in life, you are choosing to feel good! And when you start to feel good, the weight of "should" in our lives is lifted, as we maintain our well-being. Each star or area of your life is at its best when the other areas support it.

Let's take the analogy of a firework one step further. The container or shell is you. The stars are the components of your life and represent your goals. The bursting charge is the 'stuff' that surrounds the star that make it explode. This could represent many things to you—the type of environment you need to be at your best, support from friends/family, conditions you need to reach your goals, maybe circumstances or even steps you need to take in order to make your life the way that you want. The fuse ignites it. It's that light, motivation, or impetus for you to keep moving towards your balanced life. And sometimes in order to create a balanced life, you may have to learn to say 'no.'

How do you feel when you say 'no?' When you would like to, do you hear yourself think, "Well, I should…" Does this word weigh heavily on your shoulders? Have courage to extend your boundaries and say 'no.' Boundaries help you to define who you are, and how you want to live your life. Most people respect another's boundaries when communicated in a respectful way. Let yourself be free to contribute in ways you want to and choose to. Some find it helpful to say, "Let me get back to you tomorrow on that." That way, you can always take the night to sleep on it and consider if that request is something you really want to do versus something you feel obligated to do. You do have a choice.

Consider your time. Many of us have the best intentions to have a firecracking life, but sometimes it's hard! Often it is our nature to be on either extreme—doing nothing at all or committing to something beyond reason. We wind up frustrated and unwilling to try. Find the middle ground! Get a glimpse of what you can do, and focus on that! Remember a moment when you enjoyed an achievement or success in your life. Write it down! Know that you do have what it takes to be a bright firework! And when you have a day that doesn't play out the way you intended, decide that tomorrow you'll be right back on track and continuing on!

How can you begin to balance the stars in your firework? First, begin by knowing what your rounded life will look like. Image always precedes reality. Improve one area by ten per cent. Take one step. Maybe you start walking after dinner, eat a nutritious breakfast, or come home two nights a week by 5:00 p.m. Focus on one area of your life first. Then, decide to take another ten per cent improvement in another area. Each of these ten per cent improvements will make your life brighter and you feeling good. And, like compound interest, it will just keep on growing! Continue taking one step at a time towards the image you have created. Choose to give up reasons why you can't, and instead focus on why you can. Watch how it becomes easier to make choices that make you feel good, vibrant, healthy, and alert. You'll start having more energy to have fun and enjoy life. And that is what life is all about.

Define your stars, and write out one action step in one area to begin.
Job

Retirement Life

Health & Energy

Meaningful Goals

Self Knowledge

Peace of Mind

Loving Relationships

Financial Freedom

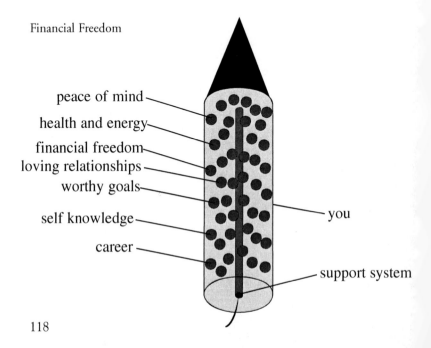

CHAPTER TEN

"What are you looking for?" Matt asked as he leaned over and turned down the radio.

"I want to make sure I brought one of my new business cards to show to Nicole," I answered. "Found one. Samantha Brooks—Artist Extraordinaire. I still like the sound of that."

"Me, too," Matt said. "So is this a little like show and tell? You guys all bring your new lives and show the teacher what you've accomplished with her sage advice?"

"Something like that," I said, adjusting the vent on the dashboard. "You know me—it's just another excuse to spend a morning drinking coffee and chattin' with the girls."

"What you three find to talk about all the time is beyond me. Jules must call you twice a day, and I know for a fact that absolutely nothing has happened in between those phone calls, but on the second call, you two talk like you haven't spoken in years!"

"Women are a strange breed." I looked at Matt out of the corner of my eye. "And women in packs are almost dangerous."

"It's a chance I'm willing to take." He leaned over for a kiss. "What time do you want me to pick you up?"

"Keep your cell on, and I'll call."

"The life of a kept man," he sighed.

"You have it pretty rough, don't ya?" I squeezed his knee. "I'll call."

"I'll answer."

I swung the door closed and started towards the café. The front door was propped open to let the morning breeze in and the smell of their house brew out.

"Hey, Jules."

"Hey, Sam. Why didn't Matt come in and say hello?"

"Are you kidding? I still don't trust you."

"I'm not a woman on the rebound anymore," Julie laughed. "I'm just a single college girl looking for a date for Friday night," she said innocently.

"Right, like you have time for extra-curricular activities." I set my purse down. "Did you finish your paper last night?"

"I have a good first draft. I'll rework some sections this afternoon."

"Ladies!" Bev wandered up to the table.

"Well, good morning, my fifty-and-looking-fabulous friend." I smiled approvingly.

"We haven't talked for a couple of weeks. How's retirement treating you?" Julie shifted her chair to allow Bev room to sit down.

"I'm dying to know the answer to that, too," Nicole had snuck in.

"Our illustrious teacher has arrived," I announced.

Julie got up and gave Nicole a hug. "Good to see you, Nic."

"It's nice to see you ladies, too." Nicole set her bag down. "I know we've all sent a couple of e-mails back and forth, I'm excited to hear the whole story about what's going on in your lives."

"But before we get started we need…" I paused.

Everyone looked around the table, and then Nicole piped up, "Coffee."

"Ah, you know me too well."

"Yes, Sam, you've proven me wrong. I guess some thing's never *do* change." Nicole smiled. "Let me join you."

"Bev, Jules, the usual?" I asked.

They both nodded and pushed some money across the table.

"It's on me." Nicole and I turned and headed towards the counter.

"So, how have you been, Sam? You look good. You look happy."

"Basically, yeah," I stopped to order the coffee. "Don't get me wrong—I still have my days when I can get discouraged. Since I've experienced a little bit of success as an artist I've gotten some weird responses from some of my friends. Not Jules or Bev," I quickly added, "but oddly enough, some of my artist friends."

"Hmmm." Nicole reached for two of the drinks. "I'm not

surprised. You're breaking out of the mold they've always known you by. If they haven't experienced a level of success yet, then they may be somewhat threatened by yours. You're not on the same playing field anymore. It's a form of jealousy, but it's more than that. You've become a mirror to them. Now that they've seen just what is possible, they are getting more and more uncomfortable with their lives. They are being forced to acknowledge just how 'stuck' they are."

"Who's stuck?" asked Julie, reaching up to grab her coffee from me.

"My friends, my other friends." I sat down.

"What do you mean 'stuck?'" Bev wrapped her hands around her steaming mug.

"What do you mean 'other friends?'" Julie smiled.

"Stuck artistically, stuck in old patterns, stuck believing what they've always believed, stuck in the status quo," I answered. "And because of that, they aren't very supportive of my 'unstuckness.'"

"That's surprising," Bev added.

"I know we did talk a little about surrounding yourself with good people, people who will encourage you during your transition and as you pursue your new life," Nicole said, looking at me, "and this is a great example of why we need to do this."

"I've got to say that it's difficult to be really excited about my life when I'm around those people. I actually downplay what I'm doing and feel guilty because my life is going so well." I paused for a sip of coffee. "I actually thought that my artistic friends would be the most supportive, the most excited for me. Boy, was I wrong."

"Being happy for another person's success is a true sign of someone who has done some of their own self-work and believes that there is enough prosperity to go around." Nicole paused. "If you have a narrow view of the universe you'll believe that fulfillment is on a first-come-first-serve basis and that there's not enough for everyone. So if someone finds fulfillment before you do, that lessens your chances of finding it. We need to remember that there is unlimited joy available to us, and if someone finds it before we do that doesn't diminish the pool available to us. There is room in this world for an unlimited amount of successful artists, entrepreneurs, CEOs, teachers, small business owners, and golf pros." She smiled at Bev.

"I've had a similar experience when I tell some people that

I'm retired," Bev said, leaning in. "Some people are very congratulatory, but others almost get mad. They'll start asking me questions like how I could possibly afford to retire so early or saying that it must be nice to lie on the sofa all day and watch TV. It's like they want me to apologize for having worked hard and planned well,"—a smile crossed her face—"and getting my proverbial kick in the butt. I was surprised the first time I got that response and then I started getting defensive, but I'm not concerned anymore with what they think or why they aren't happy for me. It's their stuff, not mine."

Nicole continued, "I know how difficult it can be to separate yourself from people like this, especially if you've had a long-term relationship, but I can't stress enough how important it is to fill your life with people who will nurture your dream, encourage you through your life transitions, and be real enough to speak the truth to you." Nicole looked at Bev. "As an aside, I know some people, mainly those going into retirement, that actually form a sort of personal advisory board."

"Sounds rather official," said Bev.

"It can be," said Nicole. "Basically they will ask a few people—I would recommend no more then six—to meet a few times a month, maybe more at the beginning, and they would literally advise them on their lives."

"Your own board of directors." Julie was intrigued with the idea.

"Yes, exactly," Nicole said enthusiastically.

Nicole went on to tell us about a client she had that was a very successful businessman in his late forties, who was looking to shift the focus of his life. He had spent the better part of his life building up his business, but along with that came long hours, extensive travel, and a more than a little stress. He decided that he wasn't ready to take up lawn bowling yet, but wanted to slow down, spend more time with family and friends, and use his skills for significance instead of success. What he did was ask five people that he respected, some from similar backgrounds and some from totally different fields of expertise and who he trusted. He laid out his goals. They would meet regularly, and give him advice on decisions he was making, both personal and business. Then they would keep him accountable. Over the course of a year he sold most of his business off to his son-in-law, kept a small stake for himself, and continued to be involved in an advisory capacity. He contacted numerous non-profit organizations that he was interested in and chose three that he would sit on boards for and offer his expertise. He still had time left over to travel with his wife and spend time with his grandchildren.

"I think he still meets with those five people every once in a while, and they make sure he is still being true to his goals and not allowing himself to fall back into old habits of letting his work consume him." Nicole reached down and turned off her vibrating cell phone.

"Personal advisory boards—I like that idea," said Julie.

"You can structure it as you like and enjoy the benefits of having a network of people that are free to be truthful with you and that you seek out advice from." Nicole looked around the table. "That was a nice detour, now tell me what's going on in your lives. Sam, I know you had shown some of your prints at the gallery down on ninth. How did that work out?"

"Not too bad. I sold one of my smaller paintings. More importantly, I got a commission from someone who came through the gallery, loved my stuff, and asked me to do three abstracts. Paid me half up front. I hope to have them done by the end of this month. If she likes them, I could see her commissioning more work since she owns a large business and we've talked about my doing some work for her offices. Could be a very lucrative deal."

"Wow, that's great, Sam." Nicole touched my arm. "Are you still working part-time from home doing the mortgages?"

"I am, although just this past month I knocked the hours down to twenty-four a week, and I only go into the office every second week."

"Are you slowly easing yourself out of the job?" Nicole asked.

"You know, I thought I was. I thought that my end goal would be to get out of the nine-to-five altogether and just live the life of an artist." I paused. "I've realized that I actually do enjoy my job, or a lot of it. Surprisingly, I'm enjoying having the mix of the left brain/right brain in my life. Sometimes the structure and routine of my job actually help me with the creative side. I feel like I have a nice balance right now, and having that regular paycheck just helps take the pressure off and allows me the freedom to paint with less stress. There might come a time when I do step out of it completely, but for now I'm pretty comfortable with the arrangement."

Nicole thought for a moment. "That's a healthy realization. I think that sometimes people see their dreams as an all-or-nothing choice. They think that they won't be happy unless they are doing it full-time. That's not always the case. For some people, they just need to integrate their dreams into their lives better, but not necessarily at the expense of everything else."

"Like I said, it may change down the road, but for now I'm enjoying the diversity." I sipped my coffee. "Oh yeah, and I'm teaching two beginners painting classes at a community center near my house and...," I paused for effect, "I just rented out my own studio space that I can move my painting stuff into next week!"

"You actually did it!" Julie practically leaped over the table.

"I did. I wasn't sure if I could afford it. It seemed like such a luxury, but winter is coming, and painting in Matt's garage is going to get a little chilly." I clenched my teeth. "So, I just started asking around and one of my students gave me a lead on the place and it was in my price range, ten blocks from my house, and has lots of natural light. I had to scoop it up. I feel like a real painter now."

Nicole smiled. "You always were; now you just have a venue."

Julie poked Bev. "You go next."

"Alright." Bev straightened up in her chair. "Well, the last few months I came to the conclusion that retiring was a lot harder than I thought it would be."

We all laughed.

"Change is never easy." Nicole shook her head. "Am I right girls?"

We all nodded.

Bev continued, "I guess I just assumed that it was a natural part of life so everything would come, well, naturally. I was wrong. I hadn't counted on having to adjust absolutely everything in my life. I had to really redefine myself."

"Have you been successful with that?" Nicole asked.

"I think so," replied Bev. "It did take me a while to figure out what it was that I enjoyed or was good at. After decades of doing things for my family, my boss, my clients, I had to stop and really think about what it was that I wanted to do."

"How did you do that?" asked Nicole.

"First of all, I had to practice some extreme self-care. I went through a period of time when I was feeling guilty for being home while my husband was still working, so I tried to compensate by making him two hot meals a day, picking up his dry cleaning, doing his filing, keeping the house immaculate. I was more tired than when I had a full-time job!"

" I hope you snapped out of that," Julie said quickly.

"Thankfully, I did." Bev slid her finger around the rim of her mug. "But I didn't want to slip into just lounging around the house all day, so I decided I had to do what you had mentioned about having a loose schedule of my week. But before I did that I took a personal retreat."

"Nice. What did you do?" asked Nicole

"I took two days at a little bed and breakfast and did lots of reading. I looked through old photo albums. I did some journaling, and I just spent time thinking about who I was and who I wanted to be. I took my calendar along and imagined what I could fill my days with. I brainstormed a bunch of ideas. I even did a couple of rough drafts and listened to how I felt when I looked at the squares on the calendar filled with activities."

"Excellent idea, Bev." Nicole smiled.

"Now I have a schedule that includes time with my grandkids, and entertaining once a week. I do a yoga class Mondays and Wednesdays. Last month I got some exercise by canvassing for the cancer society, and I'm also volunteering at an elementary school once a week, reading to kids who are learning English as a second language. I'm loving it."

"I know you had to lay down some ground rules around your grandkids, though," Julie piped in.

"How so?" asked Nicole.

"I became the convenient babysitter since now I didn't have *anything else* to do." Bev rolled her eyes. "So I had to be firm about what days I was available and started saying no to last-minute requests to watch the kids for *just an hour*. I love my grandkids, but they could easily become my second career if I'm not careful!"

"Sounds good. Has Gord adjusted as well?" Nicole asked.

Bev smiled. "Yes, my good husband has been along for the roller-coaster ride and has been very patient with me. Just last week he said he was kinda getting used to having me around the house more. I think our relationship has adjusted well, although we did have our struggles. He is eternally grateful to you for your help."

"Well, tell him, 'You're welcome.' Looks like you're up." Nicole looked at Julie.

"I guess so." Julie put her cup down. "Where to begin?"

"Hit the high points, Jules." I smiled at her, rolling my eyes.

"Okay, okay." Julie took a breath and looked at Nicole. "I think we left off with me enrolling in school and moving in with my sister, correct?"

"Correct," Nicole agreed.

"Well, I'm currently taking a couple of upgrade classes, going to full-time when the new semester starts, and I've been at my sister's for almost two months now."

"How is that arrangement working out?" Nicole shifted in her seat.

"I must say that I was a little nervous about it when we first moved in." Julie grimaced. "It's a tight space and I hadn't been that close with my sister the last few years, so that was concerning to me." Julie paused to think. "She really came through for me, though. She stepped in and has been hugely, emotionally supportive, great with the kids, and just such a comfort for me."

"So the sacrifice of space has been worth it?" asked Nicole.

"More than worth it," Julie nodded. "I wouldn't trade this time for anything. It's strange how, through these really bad circumstances, such a neat thing, like our rejuvenated relationship, has come out of it."

"Life has a funny way of disguising great gifts in the wrapping of tragedy." Nicole swished the last of her coffee in the bottom of her cup.

"So I'm not sure if there's been lots of huge outward, positive changes, but I've definitely had some inward 'a-ha moments.' Julie glanced up at me. "I'm becoming acutely aware of how important it is to invest yourself into your family and family-of-choice. Having to dramatically downsize my lifestyle has helped to clarify what's important. Going to the park with my kids or enjoying a cup of tea in the morning with my sister has brought me more pleasure than any new car ever did. I'm giving a new definition to 'the good life.'"

"Excellent." Nicole looked intently at Julie. "You've learned a lesson that many people never do. It's an old cliché that money can't buy happiness, and I'm not a big fan of poverty, but it's all in where you place value and on what. I know a lot of rich people who live like they are poor and a lot of poor people who live like they are rich. Wealth is an attitude, and I always urge people to hold onto possessions loosely and people tightly."

"Sometimes less is more," Julie laughed, "because I have less house, less cars, less bills, I have more time, more head space, and more happiness. And, hey, I know this won't last forever. Once I get through school, I have plenty of money-making years ahead of me. For right now I'm going to enjoy my simple life."

"Tell her about your part-time job, though," I urged.

"Right. I forgot. My first day of school I'm hanging in the hallway waiting for my first class to start when I see this bulletin board full of notices, and I find this ad for typing."

"Typing?" Nicole scrunched her face.

"Yeah, like typing papers for students. I call the number, and they want me to go in and do a typing test that afternoon. I ace the test, if I do say so myself," Julie smirked, "and they offer me a job on the spot, starting immediately. I get five dollars a page, and I can take on as much or as little as I'd like. It's perfect. I made almost five hundred dollars last month."

"That's great, Julie. You look happy—you all do." Nicole scanned the table.

"Even more than happy. I think we're all living genuinely, with a focus, with clarity," said Julie.

"It's still a process though," I interjected. "I'm still discovering new things about myself, if I pay attention, and I'm still very susceptible to slipping back into my old, bad habits if I'm not careful."

"Years of ingrained thought can't be eliminated overnight," Nicole agreed, "but you ladies are so far ahead of the average person that I think I can say with confidence that there's no way you can't succeed. You've done the hard work and you are much more self-aware, so this new reality that you're building for yourselves will become more and more natural to live in."

"It can take a while to create a new 'normal' can't it?" I asked.

"It can, but you have the tools now to simply do the upkeep on your 'normal.'"

"And we can't thank you enough for giving us those tools," said Julie.

"Not to mention a belt."

Everyone looked at me out of the corner of their eyes.

"That didn't come out right. I meant the tool belt."

Everyone smiled.

"It's been a pleasure working with all of you, and always remember what I said…"

"You can't have life change until you're ready to change your life!" I said enthusiastically.

"Close enough."

Everyone laughed and contemplated one more cup of coffee.

WORKBOOK:

Create your summary page for yourself:
What is your secret wish for work or retirement?

List your top four values:

1.

2.

3.

4.

Write out your top skills and/or talents:

1.

2.

3.

4.

Have you started your happy file? What do you have in it?

Write down your likes and dislikes in work.

Who are the people that support you?

What are your standards?

In what area do you need to say no?

Where do you need to be more motivated? Or confident? Write down one step that you can take towards that.

Write down two affirmations.

What is your definition of success?

List two N.E.E.D.S (not evident each day)

1.

2.

List the qualities that identify you as having healthy self-esteem or personal well-being.

Are you complacent? How? What will you do about it?

What are your activities for fun, retirement, and self-care?

What area in your Firework of Life will you begin with?

List your goals for your next career or retirement life. Put a date on them!

What are your identified career options?

Retirement: Putting it together

- ideas for fun
- family/friends
- skills/talents/abilities
- community involvement
- life purpose/mission
- what new groups interest me?
- what I currently enjoy doing
- favorite childhood activities
- what I want to learn
- school, sports, home, and friends
- what I can do for under $10
- projects
- success definition
- hobbies
- volunteer

You can re-define your role and ENJOY life!

Career Planning: Putting it together

- lifestyle
- who am I?
- who do I know
- environment
- what do I really want?
- culture
- ideal day
- skills/talents/abilities
- temporary or contract work
- values
- peak moments
- community
- vision
- goals
- satisfiers/disatisfiers

Create your plan a, b, c. Determine obstacles that could get in the way. How can you overcome them? Who can support you?

NOW PICK A PLAN

and GO FOR IT!

Know you have other plans in place should the first one not work out. It is ok to change your mind, or to have an experience that doesn't work out as hoped. Sometimes it means choosing a path and then determining if you should stick with it or go with another option. Allow your permission to do so! With careful planning, and thoughtful introspection, your first choice will likely be the best choice for you.

To succeed in Retirement and Career planning the bottom line is to:

know yourself

+

research, planning, wise choices and decisions

+

courage

= a career and life that fulfills what your definition of success is!

and remember: preparation + opportunity = success

Be courageous   Live juicy   Amaze Yourself

EPILOGUE

"So you can stop by the travel agent on the way to Terry's?" I reached into my bag to ensure I had brought my wallet.

"No problem." Matt pulled the car in front of the coffee shop and put it in park. "So we've narrowed it down to mountain-biking in Costa Rica or whitewater-rafting down the Grand Canyon, right?"

"I think we have radically different ideas of the honeymoon concept." I straightened up in my seat. "As your new bride and queen of our castle, I expect to be treated as such. Accordingly, I do not want to be expending energy portaging a raft or scraping rain-forest mud off my calves." I leaned in close to him. "There's plenty of other ways to create excitement." I kissed him.

"The honeymoon suite on the Pacific Princess it is." Matt smiled and kissed me back. "Pick you up at your place around three o'clock?"

"Yup." I pushed open the door.

"Till then, Mrs. Byrne." He reached for the gear stick.

"Not so fast," I leaned back in. "I haven't decided if I want the same name as your mother."

Matt frowned.

"We'll talk about it," I promised.

"I'm sure we will." He shifted into drive, and I closed the door.

As I walked up to the door of the coffee shop I smiled as I thought about how fortunate I was to have found my Mr. Right after so many Mr. Not-Likelys. I stepped into the room and the smell of fresh coffee hit me like a warm blanket. I noticed Bev already sitting at a corner table flipping through a magazine. The three us had not been able to get together as regularly as we used to with Julie's school schedule and homework load, my teaching commitments, and Bev's usual level of activity. I found it hard to believe it had been ten months since we had all seen Nicole. I was really looking forward to seeing everyone this morning.

"Hey, you." I snuck up on Bev.

"Hey!" She stood up and gave me an extended hug. "How are you, Sam?"

"Tired. This wedding is going to be the death of me," I sighed and sat down.

"Wait till the marriage starts!" Bev sat.

"It always starts out as 'just a few friends and family' and then turns into everyone on his rugby team from high school and all of my third cousins twice removed on my mother's side." I reached in my bag for my wallet.

"And how are you doing?"

"Before you start that conversation…" Julie and Nicole had just stepped in.

"Jules! Nicole!" Bev and I stood and hugs and greetings ensued.

Deciding to get our java before sitting back down, we all headed up to the counter. The small talk of children, husbands, and my impending wedding were the hot topics. Slipping back to the table, I felt the dichotomy of the situation—seeming as though we had met only yesterday while realizing that so much had happened in the last many months.

"Of course, I am dying to hear what's going on in everyone's lives." Nicole's eyes widened with enthusiasm. "Bev, how's retirement treating you? Everything you thought it would be?"

Bev thought a moment. "I really think that it's just now starting to feel 'normal,' like my life, like I'm not just on vacation or hiatus from work."

"Takes a while to let yourself truly accept this new life," Nicole added.

"That's for sure. I never expected the strong feelings I'd experience even months after being laid off." Bev paused. "Even talking through a lot of it with you, I still had days of feeling so sad that my career had ended that way. I was hurt and let down and unprepared to be forced into this decision."

"Do you think you're past that now?" asked Julie.

"Yeah, I think so. I realized that I was wasting a lot of energy being mad about something I couldn't change instead of accepting it and making the best of it," Bev said.

"So any other challenges along the way?" Nicole asked.

"Probably finding balance," answered Bev, "balance between having a healthy routine and having lots of free time. Just being flexible and open to new things that come my way."

"And the husband?" Nicole asked jokingly.

Bev smiled. "Yes, the husband. I hate to put him into the 'challenges' category, but we've certainly had to work through a few things. I think we've both settled into a level of comfort. We're getting used to seeing more of each other, and we're pretty good at sensing when the other person just needs to be left alone, so we'll either hide ourselves in our separate corners of the house or find an excuse to get out for an hour of two."

"Communication is pivotal," said Nicole before sipping from her mug.

"And I have been spending some time really developing my new love, gardening and landscaping," Bev said excitedly. "Been reading lots of books, took a class and a weekend workshop on it and was even offered a part-time job!"

"Are you kidding?" I said.

"Nope, but not sure what I'll do yet," said Bev. "Gord and I still need to talk it through. I'd love the work, and the little extra money wouldn't hurt, but it would be hard for me to be tied down in the summer when we like to travel. I'll have to see, but it was flattering just to be asked. I guess this old dog still has a few new tricks left in her!"

"There was never any doubt." Nicole looked over at Julie. "So what about you, Julie? What's happening in your world?"

"Well," Julie started, setting her coffee cup down, "I have experienced my share of challenges, so to speak." She glanced at me, and I smiled knowingly. "First of all, let's just say that the honeymoon ended with my sister sooner than I thought it would."

"Fight?" Nicole asked.

"Between me and her, between our children, between our dogs," Julie sighed.

"Ouch," Nicole winced.

"I was a little naïve to think I would be anything less than a complete bear to live with for a few months." Julie looked down. "I was grieving the loss of my marriage, adjusting to being a single mom, selling my house and moving, and going back to school. It was crazy. I take full responsibility for that mess."

"Are you still living there?" asked Nicole.

"Nope, just got my own place last month," said Julie. "I didn't leave without patching things up with my sister, though. We had some good heart-to-hearts, and she understood that my anger had very little to do with her. She was just the convenient punching bag."

Nicole nodded her head. "No hard feelings?"

"No. Now that we've had some time apart, we've started rebuilding and enjoying each other's company again" Julie paused. "Other challenges have been career orientated."

"I know you're still in school," said Nicole.

"Yes, and most days enjoying it," said Julie. "I just wonder sometimes if it's worth it."

"Worth it?" asked Bev.

"Worth the time, the effort, the money, the sacrifices." Julie let the frustration slip into her voice. "I'm not sure the end result will be worth it all. Not to mention, I'm not even sure what I want the end result to be. I've thought about changing my major about twenty times! From when I first started college, the world is full of new jobs, different careers. Did I choose the right path? What if I get to the end and don't really like the career I'm stuck with?"

"I don't feel we are ever really stuck with our choices," Nicole piped in. "If you don't like what you've got, simply make another choice." She paused a moment seeing Julie's discomfort. "I don't want to oversimplify this. I know you don't want to get to graduation and then have to start over again in a totally different field. You just can't look at every decision as final, with no room for some changes or adaptations. In the case of education, I never see it as a means to an end, but rather a door to more choices that you may not have had without it."

"I guess I don't want to be stuck with the label that will be on my diploma," Julie said.

"Only you can label yourself." Nicole leaned over and

touched Julie's arm. "And your label may or may not have anything to do with the designation on your degree."

"And our labels are always changing," Bev jumped in. "When your kids are young your label may be primarily 'mother'; right now, it's 'student'; when you graduate it may be 'CEO' for a while or maybe 'entrepreneur.'"

"Your right, I know." Julie gazed into her coffee cup. "I don't even have the degree yet, and I'm feeling the pressure to use it! To make something of my life because I have it."

"You have another whole year to make decisions anyway," I added.

"Aahh." Julie took a deep breath and leaned back in her chair. "Thanks, ladies, I needed that."

"And then there was, Sam." Nicole looked over at me. "Let's hear your story, ma'am."

I glanced at Julie out of the corner of my eye.

"Go on, tell her. Everything," Julie nudged me.

"Well, let's just say I almost took a step back, a gigantic step back." I looked rather sheepish.

"Hmmmm ... go on," Nicole urged.

I looked up. "I had a few slow months and just about threw in the towel."

"Your painting sales had a slump?" asked Nicole.

"Yes, and I was in between teaching gigs. I had my studio rent to pay, and, well, I suppose I just got discouraged, started questioning my decision to cut back so many of my hours at my 'real' job. Then Matt and I decided to buy a house and some easy money was looking pretty good to me."

"Do you honestly think it would have been 'easy' money?" Nicole tilted her head. "Do you know how *hard* it would have been to pay for that 'easy' money?" She used her fingers to form the quotation marks around the easy for emphasis.

"Part of it was, I felt selfish," I continued. "It wasn't just my life anymore. I want to be an equal contributor in the marriage and don't want Matt to have to finance my dreams."

"Why not?" Bev piped in. "If he's marrying you, he's marrying your dreams. He knows that. Have you talked to him about this?"

"Sort of." I fidgeted in my seat. "He says he doesn't want me to give up the studio or go back to work more hours. I believe him, but…"

"But what?" Julie asked.

"But…," I stammered.

"But you want to use him as a convenient excuse to bow out of the hard work of staying the course of your new life." Nicole paused only for a second and added, "And then ten years from now you can blame him for your not being able to fulfill your dream. Easy out."

Everyone stopped at the table.

Then Julie raised her glass. "Good answer!" Everyone joined in, "Here, here!"

"Yeah, I guess…" I didn't look up.

"Guess, nothing. She nailed it." Bev raised her eyebrows.

I slowly raised my head and said, "I shall think and meditate on your wise counsel."

"That's all I ask," Nicole nodded.

It looks like we have once again saved the world, or at least our worlds, from the brink of disaster." I smiled and set my glass down. "Thanks, Nicole."

"It has been such a pleasure meeting with you, and it's exciting to see where your journeys will take each of you. Remember that it never really ends, that life is simply one chapter after another. Just when you get to the end of one, you turn the page to discover another whole chapter. It is always, to be continued…"

During that ten months…

What if Sam doesn't sell a painting? Or she actually dislikes her switch to painting part-time?

Coaching is all about taking someone where they are now, finding out where they want to go, and determining the steps required in between to get them there. Life changes are sure to bring some unplanned scenarios or surprises. With careful planning, some of these can be thought out in advance. Sam has saved six to twelve months of salary to cover some low sales periods. She has been spending time networking with other galleries to broaden her visibility. Taking a night class has given her further expertise on style, and she has identified a target market for her work. She can expand with different pictures, designs, etc., to appeal to this target market. She has also cut her expenses, lives simply, and forgets about eating out until she is established.

Bev is having a hard time being at home with her husband. She is sometimes bored, feels strange without a business card, and is just having some difficulty adjusting to retirement life.

What should she do? How many of us can remember the *best* holiday we have ever had. Or the best *time* in our life! Just like you broke down aspects of work that you liked and didn't like, think about these times in your life. When Bev does that, she can further define activities, people, and plans that she will enjoy. Once she gets immersed in something new, her sense of purpose, and accomplishment will improve and she will begin to enjoy herself more.

As far as her husband goes … I'm not touching that one! OK, she could finish that spare room in her house to create a room of her own, a sacred space that is just hers. Maybe they need to talk about what is bugging them, or her. Is it something he is doing? Or does she just need some time on her own in the house? Maybe that's when he could be off doing his favorite activity. Communication is *key* here!

What if Julie can't stand living with her sister? Has a big fight? Can't decide on a career?

She should brainstorm what her possible alternatives are—living arrangements, job-search techniques, and books to read. She needs to determine whether she was actually in the perfectionist's syndrome, afraid of making the wrong decision, and therefore not making one at all. And what is perfect about that? Nothing. Once that is realized, then perfectionists can be free to make a well-thought-out and researched decision.

As far as her sister goes, can she make amends? Talk about it? Make some concessions to work it out? Can she afford a place of her own? What would be a good target date for that to take place?

We will all have crossroads appear throughout our lives; some obvious, some not so. Many of them, at first glance, look to be dead-ends when really they are new beginnings. We need to choose boldly. Choose relationships that are healthy not harmful, choose careers that are stimulating not static, LIVE lives full of joy and juice!

About the authors:

SHERRI OLSEN, B.A. - Author

A Professional Career and Life Coach, Sherri Olsen's experience includes searching for satisfying work in a corporate environment before launching into a career to enable others to do the same. She has coached people who have been downsized, considering retirement, or want a new career. She combines this with a practical approach to job search strategies including networking, resume writing and interview skills. She has facilitated courses in career transition, wellness and corporate coaching.

Sherri has a B.A. in Psychology and certifications from a variety of training and assessment organizations. She has completed her Professional Coach Certification from CoachU University, and is a member of Coachville.com.

Sherri can be reached at 1-866-3-coach-9 / 403-519-5998 or visit her website at www.sherriolsen.com.

VAL LIESKE - Author

      Val is a recovering banker who after being down-sized out of her career and with a little help from her Life Coach, decided to live out her dream of being an artist. This is her first, of possibly, many books. She recently started a community theatre called Fire Exit Productions. Val is also a playwright, an actor, director, producer and coffee drinker. Through her new company "Java Juice Communications" she hopes to continue to create and to further her new found passion of helping others discover and live out their dreams.

Acknowledgements:

"The printing of this book signifies the end of the first year of my new life. It has been a difficult journey and a grand adventure. I could not have imagined how radically different my life would be twelve months ago. I am not alone on this pilgrimage, though. I have many cheerleaders and confidants that have traveled with me and kept me on course.

First, my co-author, Life Coach and friend, Sherri. You helped change my mind, which changed my life. You believed in me in the most tangible way, by asking me to write a book with you! Keep using your power for good.

To my many amazing friends (you know who you are), that saw something in me that I hadn't yet seen in myself. I am blessed with the most patient, passionate and inspiring friends. Just being around you all, makes me want to be better. This book is for you.

My family, who are still a little suspicious of my new life, but encouraging just the same. Don't wait too long to integrate your dreams into your reality."

Val Lieske

"When the student is ready, the teacher appears. Enter Val, ex-banker, wanna be writer and actor. She has created a wonderful story full of characters we can all relate to. My goal was to offer sound coaching principles in a fun way. Val has done this! Plus, she has opened her own theatre company, sold her one act play, written, produced, directed, and acted in another. It was so COOL to see her perform at the engineered air theatre in Calgary. Check out www.fireexit.ca for Val's theatre company. It is very satisfying to watch someone go after their dream. Val, you rock!

Thank-you to my friends and family for their support when I took my leap of faith out of corporate world and into my own business. You have listened (yes, I know A LOT) and encouraged me. I am lucky to be surrounded with so much love."

Sherri

To our editor Jay Winans, Blue Pencil editing, Jon Lyne Book Layout, and Deneen Tedeschini, Chilipepper Graphic design...we appreciate your AWESOME work!

Val and Sherri

References:

Sandy Vilas   www.coachu.com

Tad James Neuro Linguistic Programming Master Practitioner Training, Hawaii 2000

Brian Tracy, Psychology of Achievement Course, Calgary 1999

Thomas Leonard, www.coachville.com

To Order:

To order books or for information on personal coaching
or group workshops, please contact
Crossroads Coaching
10506 Rockyledge St. NW
Calgary, AB T3G 5N2
coach@sherriolsen.com 403-282-8467
www.sherriolsen.com

Break Free From Daily Grind

group coaching via telephone

Finding Work that works
Retire Ready
Live Juicy

Contact Sherri 1-866-3-coach-9
or
coach@sherriolsen.com
Receive one free individual coaching call when you join!

Free Coach's Comments e-newsletter
email sherriolsen-subscribe@yahoogroups.com
Full of tips, coaching and stories!